HOW TO PASS

VERBAL REASONING TESTS

3RD EDITION

Harry Tolley • Ken Thomas

KOGAN PAGE

London and Philadelphia

Publisher's note

Every possible effort has been made to ensure that the information contained in this book is accurate at the time of going to press, and the publishers and authors cannot accept responsibility for any errors or omissions, however caused. No responsibility for loss or damage occasioned to any person acting, or refraining from action, as a result of the material in this publication can be accepted by the editor, the publisher or any of the authors.

First published in 1996 by Kogan Page Limited
Second edition 2000
Third edition 2006

120 Pentonville Road
London N1 9JN
United Kingdom
www.kogan-page.co.uk

525 South 4th Street, #241
Philadelphia PA 19147
USA

© Harry Tolley and Ken Thomas, 1996, 2000, 2006

The right of Harry Tolley and Ken Thomas to be identified as the authors of this work has been asserted by them in accordance with the Copyright, Designs and Patents Act 1988.

ISBN 0 7494 4666 8

British Library Cataloguing-in-Publication Data

A CIP record for this book is available from the British Library.

Library of Congress Cataloging-in-Publication Data

Tolley, Harry.
   How to pass verbal reasoning tests / Harry Tolley and Ken Thomas.—
3rd ed.
      p. cm.
   ISBN 0-7494-4666-8
   1. Verbal ability—Testing. 2. Reasoning (Psychology)—Testing.
   3. Employment tests. I. Thomas, Ken, 1939– II. Title.
BF463.V45T65 2006
153.9'3—dc22
                            2006001918

Typeset by JS Typesetting Ltd, Porthcawl, Mid Glamorgan
Printed and bound in Great Britain by Creative Print and Design (Wales), Ebbw Vale

Contents

Introduction		1
1	**A brief guide to tests**	4
	What are tests?	4
	Why do employers use tests?	5
	How can tests help you?	6
	Do tests discriminate?	7
	What are practice tests?	7
	What types of practice tests are available?	8
	What skills are being tested in different types of test?	9
	Which versions of English are assessed in verbal reasoning tests?	10
	How important is it to do well on selection tests?	11
2	**How to prepare for tests**	13
	Can practice tests make a difference?	13
	How to perform to the best of your ability on tests	14
	How to use the practice tests	15
	What do your practice-test scores mean?	17
	How to make use of feedback from practice tests	18
	Other things you can do to improve your verbal reasoning skills	19
	Online testing	22

3 **Taking real tests** 24
What to do when taking real tests 24
How to record your answers 25

4 **Verbal usage tests** 27
Introduction 27
Verbal usage tests 29

5 **Word swap tests** 56
Introduction 56
Word swap tests 58

6 **Word links tests** 67
Introduction 67
Word links tests 68

7 **Hidden sentences tests** 77
Introduction 77
Hidden sentences tests 79

8 **Sentence sequence tests** 85
Introduction 85
Sentence sequence tests 87

9 **Text comprehension tests** 104
Introduction 104
Text comprehension tests 106

10 **Verbal logical reasoning tests** 129
Introduction 129
Verbal logical reasoning tests 133

Answers 145
Verbal usage tests 145

Word swap tests	146
Word links tests	149
Hidden sentences tests	152
Sentence sequence tests	155
Text comprehension tests	157
Verbal logical reasoning tests	158

Introduction

A large number of organizations use tests as part of the process by which they select their personnel for either employment or training. For many people, therefore, selection tests can represent a serious hurdle, which they must overcome in order to gain access to a job or an opportunity to develop their career.

Unfortunately, many applicants fail these tests for reasons that are avoidable and, as a result, do not demonstrate their true potential to prospective employers. Common reasons why people under-perform on selection tests include:

■ nervousness;
■ lack of familiarity with the types of questions they are expected to answer;
■ pressure, which results from having to work quickly and accurately under test conditions;
■ poor test techniques.

Careful and systematic preparation for a test, including the use of practice tests like the ones provided here, can help to avoid these causes of failure – and the ensuing sense of disappointment and thwarted ambition.

The aim of this book, therefore, is to inform readers about selections tests in general and to offer guidance on how they might prepare themselves for taking them. The greater part of the book, however, is devoted to the provision of practice tests of the type known as 'verbal reasoning' or 'literacy' tests. These are commonly used for selection purposes to establish how competent the applicants are in their use of English. Selection for the police service, for example, includes a verbal logical reasoning test similar to the ones provided in Chapter 10. Examples of other types of verbal reasoning tests include 'word links', 'hidden sentences' and 'sentence sequences', which in their different ways seek to test the candidates' 'word power', ie their ability to read and comprehend the written word. Quite clearly, this is an area of competence a person needs to have in order to function effectively in a wide range of settings, including jobs in which they are required to read documents and write reports.

The verbal reasoning practice tests provided in this book have been developed for use with people who are preparing for selection tests. Our work with candidates studying for such tests has shown that practice can lead to significant improvements in performance. In particular, candidates who have previously failed a selection test have a much better chance of passing when they take it a second time if they have used practice tests.

Use of the practice tests provided here should enable you to:

- become familiar with the demands of different types of verbal reasoning tests commonly used for selection purposes;
- learn to work effectively in circumstances in which you will feel the 'pinch of the problem' with regard to time pressure;
- improve your test techniques so that you become less prone to making the 'silly mistakes' that can cost you valuable marks under test conditions.

The feedback you will receive from your performance on the practice tests should help to boost your self-confidence. This in turn should reduce your anxiety, nervousness and tendency to panic when confronted with a real test.

However, to succeed you will need to be well motivated, to take practice seriously and work hard to identify and address your weaknesses as they are diagnosed by the analysis of your results. If you experience serious difficulty in coping with the tests it does not mean that you are a failure and that you will never be able to succeed. It probably means that you need to build up your basic literacy skills (communication skills) before you continue to work on the practice tests prior to taking a selection test. If that is the case, the practice tests will have helped you to identify a learning need that you must address before you can make real progress. Suggestions are offered in Chapter 2 for things you can do to help yourself develop your verbal reasoning skills. However, you may need to supplement those learning activities by attending a course or courses to help raise your standard of basic literacy. You should find that such courses are available at your local Further Education College or Adult Education centre.

A brief guide to tests

The aim of this chapter is to provide you with a brief guide to tests so that you are able to understand what tests are; why they are used by employers; how they can help you; what practice tests are (and how they differ from real tests); what practice tests are available in this series of books; and what skills are being tested by different types of test.

What are tests?

Tests are designed to assess how good people are at certain things, often as a basis for predicting their future performance. Those that are designed to measure mental abilities are usually called 'cognitive tests', 'psychometric tests' or 'intelligence tests'. In the past the latter were widely used to select children for different types of schooling (eg grammar, technical and secondary modern). Since this was often done at the age of 11, such tests became known as the '11-plus'. The tests that are used by employers to choose people for jobs or for training are known as 'selection tests'. Such tests often seek to establish the aptitude people have for certain kinds of work and to measure their levels of competence in work-related skills. They may also include 'personality tests', which are designed to measure aspects of your personality that an employer considers to be significant. It may be important, for example, for them to know if you are the kind of person who can stay calm but alert in the conditions that prevail in the workplace. Personality and emotional intelligence tests help them to choose the people who they think are suited to the job.

To ensure the fairness, consistency and reliability of the results, such tests should be:

- taken under standardized conditions including strict adherence to time limits;
- administered by someone who has received the necessary training and has been certified as competent;
- objectively marked, eg through the use of an electronic scanning machine.

All of the selection tests used by employers will have been put through rigorous evaluation trials before being put into practice. When you take a real test you will find that it comes complete with carefully worded instructions and examples that tell you what you have to do to tackle it correctly. The practice tests provided in the later chapters of this book are all preceded with guidance of this kind, which you will need to read very carefully before you attempt any of the tests. Make a habit of reading test instructions carefully and working through the examples *on all occasions*, even when you think you are familiar with them already. You will find that in real tests you are usually allowed time to do this before the test begins – don't waste it!

Why do employers use tests?

The use of tests in personnel selection is based on the assumption that people who do well in the test will succeed in the job for which they have applied. Employers use selection tests, therefore, to choose people who they think are best suited for the job they have on offer. Usually the tests they use are part of a wider set of selection procedures, which will usually include an application form or curriculum vitae (CV) and an interview. Some posts even require attendance for a whole day or more at an assessment centre during which the performance of the candidates is evaluated on a whole series of job-related exercises. For example, a group decision-making or problem-solving exercise may be used to assess whether or not the candidates are capable of functioning effectively in teams. Tests are also used by employers to match their workers to the type of development training that is most suitable for them. Since the selection of personnel is a time-consuming and costly business, tests are often used in the early stages of the process to filter out unsuitable candidates, ie those who lack the necessary attributes to succeed in the job in question. This is particularly the case with large organizations, which have to deal with many applications for every vacancy.

How can tests help you?

Tests like the ones provided in the books in this series can help to show what things you are good at doing, eg working with numbers (your numeracy skills), or with words (your verbal reasoning skills). They can also help you and your employer to identify those skills in which you are strong and those you need to improve. The information can then be used as the basis for your personal development planning. The feedback obtained from tests of this kind can also help you to find work that suits you because they have been designed to test the skills and abilities that are used in the job.

Do tests discriminate?

Tests are designed to be fair to all candidates and are marked objectively. Therefore, they should help to ensure that you are given equality of opportunity in the selection process irrespective of your sex, ethnicity or any disabilities you may have. This is not to say that tests do not discriminate – in fact that is one of their main purposes. However, in order to be legal this discrimination must be on the basis of ability. In other words, when an employer uses tests to select employees, the tests must differentiate between those candidates with and those without the knowledge, skills and potential relevant to the job on offer. If a test, or the way in which it is used, discriminates on the basis of a person's sex or race, it would be judged to be unfair and possibly illegal under the terms of the Sex Discrimination Act (1975) and the Race Relations Act (1976). Hence, the people who design tests and those who use them have to take care to ensure that unfair discrimination does not occur – either intentionally or unintentionally. It is for this reason that employers monitor the performance of the tests they use to ensure that they are not discriminating unfairly by having an adverse impact on, for example, women or ethnic minority groups.

What are practice tests?

The practice tests provided in this series of books are all similar to tests that are commonly used in personnel selection. They are designed to help you to prepare yourself for taking real tests. They have all been piloted prior to publication with large numbers of candidates preparing to take real tests, including those used by the police and the Civil Service. However, these practice tests have not been subjected to the same rigorous trials and statistical analyses as the actual tests used in selecting people for training or jobs. Nevertheless, they do give you the opportunity to prepare in advance for taking such tests. In particular, they should enable you to learn how to cope with the time pressures you will have to work under in test conditions. It is for this reason that the instructions preceding the practice tests given in the later chapters all include suggestions about the amount of time you should allow yourself. In each case you will find that you are advised to give yourself progressively less time as you work through the tests. This is because you should be able to work more quickly as you become familiar with the demands of a test. It will also help to simulate real test conditions where the chances are that you will be under pressure to complete all of the questions in the time available.

What types of practice tests are available?

The practice tests in this book are designed to help you develop your word power, ie, your verbal reasoning skills. The other books in this series all include practice test material. If you are interested in assessing your number skills you should consult *How to Pass Numeracy Tests* (Harry Tolley and Ken Thomas). If you want to find out about a wide range of tests and to practise them you should consult *How to Pass Selection Tests* (Mike Bryon and Sanjay Modha). If your interests are in developing your technical skills you should use *How to Pass Technical Selection Tests* (Mike Bryon and Sanjay Modha). Finally, if you would like to assess your own aptitude, not just in the skills and abilities listed above but also your personality and motivation, you should refer to *Test Your Own Aptitude* (Jim Barrett and Geoff Williams).

What skills are being tested in different types of test?

The notes given below show what skills are being tested by different types of test. If you did well on a particular type of test it may indicate that you will do well in a job that requires you to apply the skill being tested. On the other hand, if you find that you consistently achieve low scores on a particular test it may be that you would have some difficulty in coping at this stage with jobs requiring proficiency in the skill being tested. Further work on your part to develop that skill might enable you to tackle the test more successfully at a later date.

Logical reasoning tests measure a person's ability to solve problems by thinking logically on the basis of the information provided. These can sometimes be abstract problems or they can be similar to problems encountered in the work for which people are being selected. The ability to do well in this kind of test may tell you and a potential employer that you have the ability to think critically and to solve the problems that arise at work, such as deploying resources and forward planning.

Numerical reasoning tests measure a person's ability to work competently with numbers and to solve problems based on data presented in various forms such as diagrams, graphs and statistical tables. The ability to do well in this type of test is relevant to work that requires you to work with money, interpret sales or production figures, or with the numerical aspects of science and technology.

Verbal reasoning tests aim to measure a person's ability to use language and to comprehend the written word. At work this ability is relevant to tasks such as those involving reading and writing instructions, letters and reports. At a simple level they may set out to test the candidates' basic literacy, including their ability to write grammatically correct sentences and to spell and punctuate correctly. The missing words tests in Chapter 4 fall into this category. At a more advanced level, verbal reasoning tests are looking for the ability of the candidates to understand the meaning of what has been written or said. This capacity to make sense of text is what is being tested in the hidden sentences and sentence sequence tests provided in Chapters 7 and 8.

Technical tests aim to test the candidates' skills and abilities that are relevant to various kinds of employment. Typically, these tests will include those that assess the candidates' numerical reasoning, ie their ability to understand technical ideas expressed in a mathematical form. Similarly, they may include tests of diagram reasoning (involving shapes and patterns) and mechanical reasoning (dealing with how things work).

Clerical tests aim to test the candidates' clerical skills. Typically, they will require the candidates to check and classify data speedily and accurately. In the Police Initial Recruitment test, for example, potential police officers have to compare data on a printed sheet with that on a computer screen and detect the errors.

Observation tests aim to test the candidates' powers of observation. Some of these tests may overlap with those measuring clerical skills depending upon the nature of the work for which the candidates are being tested. Others may be very specific to a particular job. Prospective police officers, for example, may be shown a series of short pieces of videotape on which they have to answer questions to test their observation skills. A typical scene might include an attempt to break into a car. The candidates would be expected to have made a mental note of such details as the colour and registration number of the car and other significant pieces of information.

Which versions of English are assessed in verbal reasoning tests?

Many different versions of the English language are in everyday use. These include regional and local dialects, the formal and the informal speech people use at work, the specialist language (jargon) of different professions, and the languages used by different social and cultural groups. New technology in the form of personal computers and mobile phones has led to a proliferation of e-mails and text messages, and with them new ways of using language. All of these different versions of English have their place and their diversity contributes to the cultural richness of our pluralistic society. However, in verbal reasoning tests it is your ability to function effectively in what is known as 'Standard English' that will be assessed. This is the form of English used universally by the majority of educated English-speaking people. It is associated with grammatical correctness and accurate spelling and punctuation. Suggestions are offered in Chapter 2 of things you can do (other than taking practice tests) to improve your competence in the use of Standard English.

How important is it to do well on selection tests?

Increasingly, a good performance on tests such as the ones described above is an important step in securing employment or access to further training. It may determine, for example, whether or not you proceed to later stages in the selection process during which your suitability for employment or training will be explored further. However, it is important to put the tests into perspective. Before they offer you a job most organizations will take into consideration the other information they have about you in your 'profile' as well as your test scores. Consequently, a modest performance on a test may be offset by:

■ the strength of your formal qualifications;
■ your previous work and life experience;
■ the way you perform in an interview;

- how well you cope with any work-related tasks they may set you.

Conversely, an outstanding test score may not be sufficient to compensate for the weaknesses in a person's profile.

How to prepare for tests

The aim of this chapter is to help you to understand how practice can have a positive effect on your test results by helping you to perform to the best of your ability; give you guidance on how to use the practice tests and interpret your scores; and give you advice on the other things you can do to improve your verbal reasoning skills.

Can practice tests make a difference?

Many candidates underachieve in selection tests because they are over-anxious and because they have not known what to expect. Practice tests are designed to help you to overcome both of these common causes of failure. The practice tests provided in the later chapters of this book will help you to become familiar with common examples of the type of test known as 'verbal reasoning'. Regular practice will also give you the opportunity to work under conditions similar to those you will experience when taking real tests. In particular, you should become accustomed to working under the pressure of the strict time limits imposed in real test situations. Familiarity with the demands of the tests and working under simulated test conditions should help you to cope better with any nervousness you experience when taking tests that really matter. Strictly speaking, the old adage that 'practice makes perfect' may not apply to selection tests, but it can make a difference – for the better!

How to perform to the best of your ability on tests

Our experience over many years of preparing candidates for both selection tests and public examinations leads us to suggest that if you want to perform to the best of your ability on tests you should follow the advice given below:

- Make sure that you know what you have to do before you start – if you don't understand, ask the supervisor.
- Read the instructions carefully before the test starts in order to make sure that you understand them.
- Skim reading through this part of the test is not good enough – it can cause you to overlook important details and to make mistakes that are easily avoidable.
- Even if you have taken a test before, don't assume that the instructions (and the worked examples) are the same as last time – they may have changed. Read them as carefully as you can.
- If it helps, highlight or underline the 'command words' in the instructions ie those words that tell you what you have to do.
- Once the test begins, work as quickly and accurately as you can. Remember, every unanswered question is a scoring opportunity missed!
- Check frequently to make sure that the question you are answering matches the space you are filling in on the answer grid (more about this in Chapter 3).
- Avoid spending too much time on questions you find difficult – leave them and go back to them later if you have time.

- If you are uncertain about an answer, enter your best-reasoned choice (but try to avoid simply 'guessing').
- If you have some spare time after you have answered all the questions, go back and check through your answers.
- Keep working as hard as you can throughout the test – the more correct answers you get, the higher your score will be.
- Concentrate on the test itself and nothing else – you cannot afford to allow yourself to be distracted.
- Be positive in your attitude – previous failures in tests and examinations should not be allowed to have a detrimental effect on your performance on this occasion. In other words, don't allow yourself to be beaten before you begin!

How to use the practice tests

To get the best out of the practice tests you should read and act on the advice given below. This consists of three sets of checklists to guide you through the different stages, ie *before* you begin, *during* the practice test and *after* you have completed it.

Before you begin to do any of the tests you should make sure that:

- you have a supply of sharpened pencils, an eraser and some paper for doing any rough work;
- you have a clock or watch with an alarm, which you can set to make sure that you work within the time limit you have set yourself;
- you are in a quiet room where you will not be disturbed or distracted, with an uncluttered desk or table at which you can work;
- you decide in advance which test you are going to tackle and review what you learnt from the previous practice session;
- you understand the instructions before you begin; even though you may think that you are already familiar with them, read the instructions on how to complete the test;

- you work through the example(s) provided so that you know exactly what to do before you start;
- you know how to record your answer correctly (see below).

You should then be ready to set your timer and turn your attention to the chosen practice test.

During the practice test you should try to:

- work quickly and systematically through the items – above all, do not panic;
- move on to the next question as quickly as you can if you get stuck at any point – you can always come back to unfinished items at the end if you have time;
- remember to check over your answers if you have any spare time at the end;
- stop working as soon as the time is up (and mark the point you have reached in the test if there are any items that you have not completed).

After the practice test you should:

- check your answers with those given at the end of each chapter;
- put a tick against each question that you answered correctly and a cross next to each one you got wrong;
- add up the number of ticks to give you your score on the test as a whole;
- compare your score with those on previous tests of the same type to see what progress you are making;
- work through any items that you did not manage to complete in the test and check your answers;
- try to work out where you went wrong with any questions that you answered incorrectly.

If possible, talk through how you arrived at your answers with someone who has also done the test. Discussion of this kind can help to reinforce your learning by:

- helping you to understand why you got the wrong answers to certain questions;
- giving you a better understanding of the questions to which you got the right answers;
- suggesting alternative ways of arriving at the same answer to a question.

Discussion of this kind can help you to reach an understanding of the principles that underlie the construction of the test. In other words, you can begin to get 'inside the mind' of the person who set the questions. Working collaboratively with someone else can also help to keep you motivated and provide you with encouragement and 'moral' support if and when you need it.

What do your practice-test scores mean?

Because practice tests tend to be shorter than real ones and have not been taken under the same conditions, you should not read too much into your practice-test scores. You will usually find that the real tests you sit are more exacting because they will be:

- longer than the examples provided in this book;
- administered formally in a standardized way by a person who has been trained in their use;
- more stressful than practice tests.

Nevertheless, your practice-test scores should provide you with feedback on how your performance on the same type of test (eg missing words or hidden sentences) varies from one practice test to another, and hence what progress you are making over time. They will also give you feedback on how well you are doing on one type of test (eg word links) compared to another (eg hidden sentences), and hence what your strengths and weaknesses appear to be.

However, when trying to make sense of your practice-test scores you should remember that:

- In real tests your score will be compared with the performance of a group of typical candidates to determine how well you have done.
- The pass mark in selection tests set by employers can go up or down depending on how many applicants there are and the number of job vacancies that are available at any one time.
- Most tests are designed to ensure that very few candidates manage to get high or full marks.
- As a general rule the typical score for the majority of candidates sitting real tests will be a little over a *half of the maximum* available, though this can vary from test to test.

How to make use of feedback from practice tests

More important than your total score on a practice test is *how* you achieved that overall mark. For example, you could begin this diagnosis by making a note of the answer to the following questions:

- How many questions did you attempt within the given time limit and how many remained unanswered?
- How many of the questions that you completed did you answer correctly?

■ Where in the test were most of your incorrect answers (eg at the end when you were working in a hurry, or at the beginning when you may have been nervous or had not settled down properly)?

The answers to these questions should give you some pointers as to how you might *improve* your scores in future tests by changing your behaviour. For example, if you got most of the questions right, but left too many unanswered, you should try to work quicker next time. If you managed to answer all the questions, but got a lot of them wrong, you should try to work more accurately, even though that might mean that you have to work more slowly.

Remember, the object of the exercise is to score as many correct answers as you can in the time allowed. Thus, there is a balance to be struck between speed and accuracy. Intelligent practice and careful evaluation of your results can help you to reach the right balance for you.

Other things you can do to improve your verbal reasoning skills

Essentially, verbal reasoning tests are seeking to measure how effectively you can function in a particular language – in this case English. The different types of test are merely trying to assess particular aspects of that general ability. So, in addition to using the practice tests, you need to do as many different things as you can to increase your 'word power' or communication skills. Some practical suggestions for you to work on as part of your personal development action plan are set out below.

Before you begin to put any of them into practice you should bear in mind the need to adopt a systematic approach to the development of your verbal reasoning. You will not achieve the improvements you want to make by picking out activities at random from the checklist given below and trying them out spasmodically. You need to work consistently to a plan and to set yourself some realistic targets:

- Making a habit of reading a variety of material regularly (eg newspapers, magazines and books) is a good place to begin. Remember that the reading demands of text can vary from one item to another. For example, tabloid newspapers are generally much easier to read than the broadsheets. In order to develop your verbal reasoning skills you will need to 'push' yourself to read things that you have difficulty in coping with at first. Unfamiliar subject matter and the use of long sentences, large words and jargon can all contribute to the reading difficulty of a piece of text.
- Become an 'active' (as opposed to a 'passive') reader. You can do this by highlighting key points in the text, or by making notes in pencil in the margin. An interesting exercise you can do is to take a newspaper or magazine article on a topic that interests you and go through it underlining the 'facts' that are quoted by the writer in one colour and the 'opinions' he or she expresses in another.
- Ask questions while you are reading, eg, 'What is the writer really trying to say?', 'Is that logical?' and 'Does that make sense?'
- Get someone to ask you probing questions about your reading or to discuss it with you.
- Write summaries about what you have read.
- Play word games and do crossword puzzles. Remember that the latter can vary enormously in their level of difficulty. If you find that you can solve a particular puzzle quickly it may be time to move on to one that is more difficult.
- Make a list of any words that you frequently misspell and learn how to spell them. If you have difficulty in doing this try the 'look, cover, spell and check method' ie *look* at the word, *cover* it up, write down how to *spell* it and then *check* to see if you

managed to spell it correctly. (You can make a start by trying out the method on the following commonly misspelt words: accommodate; beautiful; disappear; friend; government; harassment; necessary; occasion; occurred; reference.)

■ Make a habit of looking up the meaning of words in a dictionary as well as how to spell them. You may be in for some surprises if you do this – familiar words often have different meanings from the one associated with them.

■ Try to get a grip of the specialist language or jargon used by different groups with whom you come into contact. For example, if someone uses a technical term with which you are unfamiliar, ask him or her to define it.

■ Make lists of synonyms (words that have the same meanings) and antonyms (words that have opposite meanings) by using a dictionary and/or a thesaurus.

■ Paraphrase (ie, put into your own words) what someone else has written or said.

■ Get someone to cut up some passages of text into segments and then jumble them up – your task is to reassemble the passages into their original sequence.

■ Get someone to type or word-process some passages of text for you in which they have left out every tenth word. Tell them to replace the missing words with a line of standard length. Your task is to read the passage and work out what you think the missing words are. In order to be 'right' it is not necessary for you to get exactly the same words as those that were used in the original. All you have to do is to find words which, when put into the empty spaces, make sense to anyone reading the passage. You can make the task progressively more difficult by choosing text that is harder for you to read and by increasing the number of words you leave out, eg every ninth as opposed to every tenth word.

■ Learn how to listen carefully to what people are saying and how they express themselves. Radio and television broadcasts (especially the former) are good sources of listening material.

As with reading matter, you should vary the types of material you listen to: try to include talks, interviews, discussions and formal debates. Listen especially for the way in which skilled and experienced speakers vary their use of language according to the circumstances and nature of their audience.

It should be remembered that the benefits you are seeking to gain from the learning activities listed above are cumulative – small improvements building on each other incrementally. It is more likely that such gains will be achieved by consistent application over a period of time measured in weeks and months rather than by a last-ditch effort just before you take an important test. Preparing for tests and examinations is a bit like training for a race – it is the fitness that you build up over the long term that enables you to 'peak' at the right time.

Online testing

You may be asked to complete your verbal reasoning tests online. There is nothing to worry about in doing electronic versions of tests. You might even find it to be more fun than by paper and pencil – many people do. Obviously we are not in a position here to prepare you for such an experience, but why not go to the web to complete a practice test or two? Three useful sites are:

www.careers.ed.ac.uk
www.bath.ac.uk/careers/development/tests
www.careers.bham.ac.uk/links/psychometric.htm

Other sites (most of which you will find listed in the three sites above) are:

The Morrisby Organization (www.morrisby.com)
Saville & Holdsworth (SHL) (www.shldirect.com)
Tests from Team Technology (www.teamtechnology.co.uk)

If you aspire to join the Civil Service, and especially the fast stream, you might find yourself being invited to attend a Civil Service assessment centre. In that eventuality you will no doubt want to practise the Civil Service Fast Stream Qualifying Test. There are two tests, data interpretation (numerical reasoning) and verbal organization (verbal reasoning), and each takes 20–30 minutes to complete. You can do these practice tests online by going to www. faststream.gov.uk and clicking on the self-assessment programme, or to the self-selection programme to check whether you are a suitable applicant in the first place.

All in all, therefore, there are plenty of online practice opportunities for you to tap into – try to take advantage of them in preparing for the verbal reasoning tests you are likely to face.

3

Taking real tests

The aim of this chapter is to give you guidance on what to do when taking real tests and the different ways you might be expected to record your answers in such tests.

What to do when taking real tests

Before taking any tests, for example as part of the selection process for a job or for training, you should:

- Find out as much as you can about the test in advance, eg ask if any examples of the types of question you will be asked are available.
- Try to get a good night's sleep before the test.
- Make sure that you get to the place where the test is to be held in good time so that you do not get anxious through having to rush.
- Ensure that you have your glasses, contact lenses or hearing aid available if you need to use them during the test.
- Inform the organization or employer conducting the test in advance about any disability you may have so that they can make the necessary arrangements for you.

At the test itself you should:

■ Listen very carefully to the instructions you are given by the person administering the test.

■ Do exactly what you are told to do.

■ Read the written instructions carefully.

■ Work carefully through any practice questions that may be provided.

■ Make sure that you understand how you are required to record your answers.

■ Ask the supervisor if there is anything that you do not understand.

■ When told to begin the test, read each question carefully before answering.

■ Work as quickly and accurately as you can.

■ Keep an eye on the time.

■ Stop working immediately when told to do so.

After the test you should avoid worrying about your test results and get on with the rest of the selection process – people are usually selected by an employer for reasons other than high test scores. When it is appropriate to do so, ask for feedback on your performance even if you are not offered the job or a place on the training scheme – it may help you to be successful the next time.

How to record your answers

In the practice tests provided here you will find that the questions and the answer boxes or spaces are presented together. However, when you take real tests you will usually find that separate question and answer sheets or booklets will be used. This is because electronic scanners or optical mark readers are often used to mark and score the test papers, especially with large organizations such as Civil Service departments and agencies.

It is essential, therefore, that your answers are presented in a form that the machine can understand. The instructions at the start of the test will usually tell you exactly how to mark your answers. For example, boxes must be marked with a dark pencil mark that completely fills the response position on the answer sheet; this is particularly the case with computer-scanned marking. Light or partial marks, ticks, oblique strokes (/) or crosses will be ignored and marked as wrong.

Some questions will ask you to mark two or more circles or boxes instead of one, so read the question carefully as an incorrect number of responses will also be marked as wrong. If you make a mistake or change your mind, use a rubber to erase all unintentional marks completely from the answer grid.

Many questions are presented in a *multiple choice* format in which you are required to choose the correct answer from the given alternatives and to record this by putting a mark against the box (or circle) of your choice. For example, if you decide that the answer to a particular question is the one labelled B, you would record your answer like this:

A O   B ●   C O   D O

If boxes were being used instead of circles and you decided that the answer to a particular question was the one labelled number 3, you would record your answer like this:

1 □   2 □   3 ■   4 □   5 □

Sometimes you are asked to record your answer by <u>underlining</u> words. Once again you should take care to follow the instructions exactly – too many or too few words underlined, or marks placed incorrectly, will lead to your answer being marked as wrong.

4

Verbal usage tests

Introduction

In this type of verbal usage test you will find sentences in which two gaps have been left, which is why they are often called 'missing words tests'. Your task is to decide which two words have been omitted. Below each sentence you will find four pairs of words, with a letter (A, B, C and D) above each pair. You have to work out which *one* of these pairs of words fits into the spaces correctly. Sometimes it is simply a question of the correct spelling of the words or their precise meaning. On other occasions it is a matter of which words to use in the construction of a sentence so that it is grammatically correct. However, in some of the items the right answer will be *'None of these'*, in which case you would record your decision by writing the letter E in the answer space provided. The two examples given below should help you to get the idea.

Example 1

Three senior officers _____ present at the internal _____.

A	B	C	D
was	was	were	were
enquirey	enquiry	enquiry	enquirey

E None of these

Answer C

In this example the subject (ie, the *Three senior officers*) is third person plural. The correct form of the verb, therefore, is *were* <u>not</u> *was*. Had the sentence read *The senior officer* (ie, had the subject been singular not plural) the first missing word would have been *was*. The second missing word is the one in which the spelling is incorrect ie, it should be *enquiry* <u>not</u> *enquirey*. Now take a look at the second example.

Example 2

During the investigation a potential witness was _____ talking to the _____.

A	B	C	D
scene	seen	scene	scene
suspect	susspect	susspect	suspect

E None of these

Answer E

In this example, with the first missing word it is not simply a case of getting the correct spelling. The right answer is *seen*, which is part of the verb in the sentence. The word *scene* is not only spelt differently but it is an object and therefore a noun. The second word is 'suspect' (not 'susspect') because of the two, it is the one that is spelt correctly. None of the alternatives A–D, therefore, offers the correct pair of words, so the answer must be E.

Four practice tests of this type are given below – with each test consisting of 25 questions. For Test 1 allow yourself 12 minutes, ie approximately half a minute per question. Work as quickly and accurately as you can. If you are not sure of an answer, mark your best choice, but avoid wild guessing. If you want to change an answer, rub it out completely and then write your new answer in the space provided. Give yourself one mark for each correct answer and make a note of your score so that you can use that information to see if you are making any progress from one to another. Remember to work carefully through any answers that you get wrong or fail to complete in the time allowed. Once you have completed Test 1 and checked your answers, you can put some pressure on yourself by reducing the amount of time you allow yourself for each test – your aim being to complete Test 4 in 10 minutes.

Verbal usage tests

Test 1

1. A section of dual _____ forming part of the outer ring road was closed due to _____ .

A	B	C	D
carrigeway	carriageway	carrigeway	carriageway
alterations	allterations	allterations	alterations

E None of these

Answer [D]

2.   The road _____ involving two vehicles was _____ by a stray dog.

A	B	C	D
acident	accident	accident	acident
coursed	caused	coursed	caused

E None of these

Answer [E]

3.   The _____ in the park happened late on _____ night.

A	B	C	D
atack	atack	attack	attack
Saterday	Saturday	Saterday	Saturday

E None of these

Answer [D]

4.   His _____ new car was a complete _____ -off as a result of the collision.

A	B	C	D
beautiful	beutiful	beatiful	beautiful
write	right	write	right

E None of these

Answer [A]

5.   After the fire the couple could not _____ their home insurance _____ .

A	B	C	D
prodduce	produce	produce	prodduce
certificate	certifecate	certifficate	certifficate

E None of these

Answer [E]

6. The patient was told that it was _____ to keep doing the _____ in order to improve his mobility.

A	B	C	D
importent exercises	importent exercices	important exercices	important exercises

E None of these

Answer [D]

7. It soon became apparent that the new _____ was a very _____ worker.

A	B	C	D
colleague competent	coleague competant	collegue competent	colleague competant

E None of these

Answer [A]

8. The staff soon found that the _____ electronic _____ were easy to use.

A	B	C	D
new diaries	knew diaries	new dairies	knew dairies

E None of these

Answer [A]

9. The policies proposed by the _____ were said by many people to be far too _____.

A	B	C	D
goverment complicated	government complecated	government complicated	goverment complecated

E None of these

Answer [C]

10.   The survey showed that the old _____ who lived alone on the estate were very _____.

A	B	C	D
poeple	people	people	poeple
lonely	loneley	lonely	lonly

E None of these

Answer [C]

11.   The missing traffic _____ was found _____ beside the stolen car.

A	B	C	D
warden	wordon	warden	wardon
unconsious	unconscious	unconcious	unconscious

E None of these

Answer [E]

12.   The pit bull _____ was said to be extremely _____ by those questioned.

A	B	C	D
terrior	terrier	terier	terior
vicious	vicious	viscious	visious

E None of these

Answer [B]

13.   _____ _____ rights are we talking about in this situation?

A	B	C	D
Who's	Whose	Whose	Who's
welfare	wellfare	welfare	wellfare

E None of these

Answer [A] X

→ whose

C

14.   At this time of year it is noticeable that the _____ is
      getting _____ each day.

A	B	C	D
wheather	whether	weather	whether
worse	worser	worser	worse

E None of these

→ worse   Answer [C] X

                                                              E

15.   The local _____ was always closed by 8.30 pm on a
      _____ evening.

A	B	C	D
garrage	garage	garage	garrage
Tuesday	Teusday	Tuesday	Teusday

E None of these

                               Answer [C]

16.   The speed limit remains at _____ miles _____ hour
      on all motorways.

A	B	C	D
seventey	seventy	seventy	seventey
per	pur	per	pur

E None of these

                               Answer [C]

17.   Do any of you _____ what has _____ to the stolen
      car?

A	B	C	D
no	know	no	know
hapened	hapened	happened	happened

E None of these

                               Answer [D]

18.   The _____ was found hidden in a bag in the top _____ of the dressing table.

A	B	C	D
revolvor	revolvor	revolver	revolver
draw	drawer	drawer	draw

E None of these

Answer [C]

19.   The officer will be _____ to other duties in _____.

A	B	C	D
transferred	transferred	transfered	transfered
August	Augaust	August	Augaust

E None of these

Answer [A]

20.   The _____ lights at a busy road junction failed for the _____ time that month.

A	B	C	D
trafic	traffic	traffic	trafic
thirteenth	thirtineth	thirteenth	thirtenth

E None of these

Answer [C]

21.   The new office _____ was paid for over a three-year period by a monthly _____ plan.

A	B	C	D
eqiupement	equipement	equipment	equippment
installment	installment	instalment	instalment

E None of these

Answer [C]

22. It was clear that the team must _____ acted in a very _____ manner.

A	B	C	D
of	have	have	of
professionel	professional	proffesional	professional

E None of these

Answer ⬚ B

23. In keeping with the new policy, an _____ _____ was invited to attend the enquiry.

A	B	C	D
independent	independent	independant	indapendant
observer	observor	observor	observer

E None of these

Answer ⬚ A

24. Given the vociferous opposition it was _____ that the _____ had been granted.

A	B	C	D
suprising	serprising	surprising	supprising
license	license	licence	licence

E None of these

→ licence   Answer ⬚ A   X
                                C

25. The school inspector reported that the results of the new examination _____ _____.

A	B	C	D
were	was	were	was
disasterous	dissastrous	disastrous	disastrous

E None of these

Answer ⬚ C

Test 2

1. Everyone involved in the incident was _____ at the hearing _____ the key witness.

A	B	C	D
their	there	they're	there
except	except	except	eccept

E None of these

Answer [ℬ]

2. The senior police _____ _____ the parents that the children would be safe.

A	B	C	D
officer	oficer	officer	oficer
asured	assured	assured	asured

E None of these

Answer [C]

3. Did the army _____ _____ the man who was injured in the incident?

A	B	C	D
sargeant	sergeant	sergant	sergeant
no	know	know	no

E None of these

Answer [ℬ]

4. The man thought to have been the _____ was _____ dead when the medical services arrived.

A	B	C	D
murdrer	murderer	murdurer	murderer
allready	allready	already	already

E None of these

Answer [D]

5. In court the _____ spoke with a very loud _____.

A	B	C	D
juge	judge	jugde	jugde
voice	voise	voice	voise

E None of these

Answer [E]

6. The _____ was very _____ whilst the barrister questioned the witness.

A	B	C	D
jury	jurey	jury	jurey
atentive	attentive	attentive	attendtive

E None of these

Answer [C]

7. The _____ said that she was horrified by the _____ made against her.

A	B	C	D
defendant	defendent	deffendant	deffendant
accusation	accusation	accusation	acusation

E None of these

Defendant

Answer [B] X

A

8. It was reported that the _____ was seen leaving the house carrying a very _____ bag.

A	B	C	D
theif	thief	theif	thief
ordinary	ordinary	ordinery	ordinery

E None of these

Answer [B]

9.　The victim's _____ were found to have been _____ with blood.

A	B	C	D
cloths	clothes	clothes	cloths
stained	stained	staned	staned

E None of these

Answer [B]

10.　It turned out that the washing _____ found in the storeroom had been _____ the previous day.

A	B	C	D
machins	machenes	machines	machines
stolen	stollen	stollen	stolen

E None of these

Answer [D]

11.　When questioned the _____ said that it was not _____ to treat him in that way.

A	B	C	D
acused	accused	acused	accused
fair	fair	fare	fare

E None of these

Answer [B]

12.　You _____ do that with so many people around because it is _____ dangerous.

A	B	C	D
can't	ca'nt	cann't	can't
too	to	two	to

E None of these

Answer [A]

13. The _____ looked very _____ on arrival at the station.

A	B	C	D
criminel	criminal	criminall	criminal
pale	pail	pail	pale

E None of these

Answer ☐ D

14. The only item taken by the _____ was the new _____ set.

A	B	C	D
burglar	burgler	burgular	burglar
television	tellevision	television	tellevision

E None of these

Answer ☐ A

15. The person who had _____ the coin onto the pitch was told that he had committed an _____.

A	B	C	D
throne	thrown	throne	thrown
ofence	offense	offense	ofence

E None of these

offence   E

Answer ☐ B ✗

16. To _____ does this pencil and notebook _____?

A	B	C	D
who	whom	whose	who
belong	belong	belong	bellong

E None of these

Answer ☐ A ✗

whose   C
belong

17.   The _____ to change the planning laws was made by
      _____.

A	B	C	D
descision	decision	desision	decision
parliment	parliment	parliament	parliament

E None of these

Answer [D]

18.   It was found that a _____ liquid had been _____ from
      the bottle.

A	B	C	D
mysterrious	mysterious	misterious	misterious
leaking	leeking	leaking	leeking

E None of these

Answer [E]

19.   The _____ dogs soon picked up the _____ left by the
      intruder.

A	B	C	D
gaurd	guard	guard	gaurd
scent	sent	cent	sent

E None of these

Answer [E]

20.   Despite its appearance to the contrary, the _____ dog
      turned out to be very _____.

A	B	C	D
strayed	stray	strayed	stray
tame	tamed	tamed	tame

E None of these

stray   D

tame

Answer [C]

21. A road accident _____ as they _____ walking down
the street.

A   B   C   D
occurred   ocurred   ocurred   occurred
was   were   was   were

E None of these

Answer D

22. It _____ long before an _____ started amongst the
group.

A   B   C   D
wasn't   wasn't   was'nt   was'nt
argument   arguement   argument   arguement

E None of these

Answer A

23. The _____ over the bank holiday weekend was very _____ .

A   B   C   D
weather   whether   weather   whether
dissapointing disappointing   disappointing   dissappointing

E None of these

Answer C

24. To _____ do you write to obtain the _____ information
about the job?

A   B   C   D
who   whom   whom   who
appropriate apropriate   appropriate apropriate

E None of these

Answer C

25.   The person's _____ from the meeting was totally _____ .

A	B	C	D
absance	absence	absance	absence
unnecessary	unecessary	unnecesary	unnecessary

E None of these

Answer ⬚ D

Test 3

1.   The _____ could not remember anything about the strange _____ .

A	B	C	D
neighbour	neighbour	nieghbour	nieghbour
rumours	rumors	rumours	rumors

E None of these

Answer ⬚ A

2.   Fortunately the _____ used in the robbery at the shop had _____.

A	B	C	D
pistal	pistal	pistol	pistol
misfired	missfired	misfired	missfired

E None of these

Answer ⬚ C

3. In keeping with company policy _____ was given to the
   people who had _____ early.

A   B   C   D
prefference   preferance   preferance   preference
arrived   arived   arrived   arived

E None of these

Answer E

4. The hospital _____ was sitting up in bed dressed in white
   _____.

A   B   C   D
patcient   patient   patcient   patient
pjamas   pjamas   pyjamas   pyjamas

E None of these

Answer D

5. The number of anniversary _____ the couple received was
   _____ overwhelming.

A   B   C   D
presents   presence   presents   presence
quiet   quite   quite   quiet

E None of these

Answer E

6. The question to be decided was who was going to _____
   the _____ at the fancy dress party?

A   B   C   D
where   ware   wear   wear
mask   masque   masque   mask

E None of these

Answer D

7.   This is the _____ _____ the robber had used to make
     his escape.

A	B	C	D
bycicle	bicycle	bycicle	bicycle
what	which	which	what

E None of these

Answer B

8.   The records show that the _____ of rain _____
     increased this year compared with last.

A	B	C	D
amount	amount	ammount	ammount
has	have	has	have

E None of these

Answer A

9.   The _____ became so seriously ill that he had to be
     _____ to another hospital.

A	B	C	D
soldior	soldier	soldior	soldier
reasigned	reassigned	reassigned	reasigned

E None of these

Answer B

10.   _____ the police officer _____ by the house.

A	B	C	D
Occasionally	Occasionally	Ocasionally	Ocasionally
past	passed	past	passed

E None of these

Answer B

11.   The _____ _____ to his heart's content.

A
drunkerd
sang

B
drunkard
sang

C
drunkard
sung

D
drunkerd
sung

E None of these

Answer ☐

12.   The pavements were very _____ the morning after the
first frosty night of the _____.

A
slippey
autumn

B
slippy
autum

C
slippey
autum

D
slippy
autunm

E None of these

Answer E

13.   The _____ driver had several _____ with her for use
in such an emergency.

A
amulance
bandages

B
ambulance
bandeges

C
ambulence
bandages

D
ambulance
bandages

E None of these

Answer D

14.   The _____ was _____ in for the staff to read during
the lunch break.

A
bulletin
brought

B
buletin
brought

C
bulletin
brouhgt

D
buletin
brouhgt

E None of these

Answer A

15. The _____ had _____ to the nearest telephone to report what had happened.

A	B	C	D
athleet	athlete	athleet	athlete
ran	runned	run	run

E None of these

Answer ☐ D

16. The new _____ was very _____ in conducting its business.

A	B	C	D
commitee	comittee	committee	commitee
efficient	effecient	efficient	eficient

E None of these

Answer ☐ C

17. The _____ who attended the incident _____ the police officer's injured hand.

A	B	C	D
docter	docter	doctor	doctor
examined	examened	exammined	examened

E None of these

Answer ☐ E

18. The constable was already _____ with a very _____ situation when a second disagreement erupted.

A	B	C	D
deeling	dealing	dealing	deeling
delecate	delicate	delecate	delicate

E None of these

Answer ☐ B

19. They had been _____ well in advance to be _____ in their attendance.

A	B	C	D
tolled	told	told	tolled
punctual	punctul	punctual	punctul

E None of these

Answer [C]

20. On closer examination the _____ at the bottom of the application form _____ to be false.

A	B	C	D
signiture	signature	signature	signiture
seemed	seemed	seamed	seamed

E None of these

Answer [B]

21. The _____ showed that there had been a _____ increase in the school's examination pass rates.

A	B	C	D
annalysis	analysis	analisys	analysis
noticable	noticeable	noticible	noticable

E None of these

Answer [B]

22. The new _____ of study at the college was highly _____ to the applicants by the Principal.

A	B	C	D
coarse	coarse	course	course
recommended	reccomended	recommended	recomended

E None of these

Answer [C]

23.   The girl was _____ upset when she heard the news about
      her _____ illness.

A	B	C	D
extremley	extremeley	extremely	extremely
father's	fathers'	fathers	father's

E None of these

Answer [D]

24.   It was her _____ to reserve her overnight _____ at a
      hotel well in advance.

A	B	C	D
practice	practise	practise	practice
acomodation	acomodation	accommodation	accommodation

E None of these

Answer [D]

25.   The report concluded that the _____ selection _____
      are unsatisfactory.

A	B	C	D
currant	current	current	currant
criteria	criterion	criteria	criterion

E None of these

Answer [C]

Test 4

1. The officer was _____ by what the examination revealed about the _____ on the car.

A	B	C	D
apalled	appalled	apalled	appalled
breaks	brakes	brakes	breaks

E None of these

Answer ☐

2. Those responsible for running the _____ have been charged with _____.

A	B	C	D
busines	bussines	bisness	business
fraud	frord	fraurd	fraud

E None of these

Answer ☐

3. The _____ that appeared in the local newspaper was _____ shocking.

A	B	C	D
advertisement	adverticement	adverticement	advertisement
extreemly	extremely	extreemly	extremeley

E None of these

Answer ☐

4. A thorough examination showed that the _____ _____ had been badly maintained.

A	B	C	D
safty equipment	safety equiptment	saftey equipment	safety equipment

E None of these

Answer ☐

5. Even his own _____ did not _____ his explanation.

A	B	C	D
daugter believe	dauhgter believe	daughter believe	daughter beleive

E None of these

Answer ☐

6. The officer's _____ of the missing witness was _____.

A	B	C	D
discription inadequate	description inadequate	discription inadaquate	description inadecuate

E None of these

Answer ☐

7. A pack of ice was put on her _____ to relieve the pain and _____ the swelling.

A	B	C	D
forhead reduce	fourhead redduce	forehead reduce	forhead redduce

E None of these

Answer ☐

8.   The doctor's prescription said that the _____ should be
      taken _____.

A	B	C	D
medecine	medicine	medicine	medecine
daily	daily	dialy	dailly

E None of these

Answer [ ]

9.   In _____ the road conditions were often _____ because
      of the weather.

A	B	C	D
February	Febuary	Febuary	February
dangerous	dangerous	dangerrous	dangerrous

E None of these

Answer [ ]

10.   It was reported in the media that a _____ had _____
      from a high security facility.

A	B	C	D
psychapath	sychopath	psychapath	psychopath
escaped	escapped	escapped	escaped

E None of these

Answer [ ]

11.   The _____ took time over its deliberations resulting in a
      long _____ before the verdict was announced.

A	B	C	D
jury	jury	jurey	jurey
weight	wait	wait	waite

E None of these

Answer [ ]

12. The _____ had just left the public _____ when the incident took place.

A
pensionner
library

B
pensioner
libary

C
pensioner
library

D
pensionner
libary

E None of these

Answer ☐

13. He had _____ long and hard with the other _____ before he finally capitulated.

A
fort
competitors

B
fought
competetors

C
fort
competetors

D
fought
compitetors

E None of these

Answer ☐

14. The younger members of the _____ were very _____ to the social worker.

A
familly
impertinant

B
familly
impertinent

C
family
impertinant

D
family
impertinent

E None of these

Answer ☐

15. The victims were _____ some _____ to aid their recovery.

A
offered
therapy

B
offered
therapy

C
oferred
therapy

D
offered
therappy

E None of these

Answer ☐

16. The long-awaited _____ was finally held _____.

A	B	C	D
trial	trial	trail	trail
yesturday	yesterday	yesterday	yesturday

E None of these

Answer ☐

17. The survey showed that on average _____ to work by public transport takes _____ minutes.

A	B	C	D
traveling	traveling	travelling	travelling
fiftey	fifty	fifty	fiftey

E None of these

Answer ☐

18. The _____ of the public concerns, which led to the _____, was unclear.

A	B	C	D
sauce	source	sauce	sourse
enquiry	inquiry	inquiry	enquiry

E None of these

Answer ☐

19. The medical examination revealed that she was _____ from multiple _____ as a result of the accident.

A	B	C	D
suferring	suffering	suffering	suferring
bruises	bruses	bruises	bruses

E None of these

Answer ☐

20. The exact _____ of the _____ overlooking the square
     was not known.

A	B	C	D
height	height	hight	hight
building	biulding	building	biulding

E None of these

Answer ☐

21. Her driving _____ was subsequently found to be _____.

A	B	C	D
licence	license	licensce	licence
invallid	invallid	invalid	invalid

E None of these

Answer ☐

22. Understandably, the victim's _____ was _____ upset
     at the news.

A	B	C	D
fianncé	fiancé	fiancée	fiancée
genuinely	genuinly	genuinly	genuinely

E None of these

Answer ☐

23. Despite its importance, it turned out to be a very _____
    _____.

A	B	C	D
plane	plain	plane	plain
document	doccument	doccument	document

E None of these

Answer ☐

24. The financial collapse of the company occurred because the
_____ had _____ all the warning signals.

A	B	C	D
accountant	acountant	accountant	acountant
ignored	ignored	ignawed	ignawed

E None of these

Answer ☐

25. The students received _____ good attendance _____.

A	B	C	D
their	there	their	there
awards	awords	awords	awards

E None of these

Answer ☐

The answers to the verbal usage tests are given on pages 145–46.

5

Word swap tests

Introduction

In this type of verbal reasoning test you are given a series of sentences in which the positions of two words have been swapped so that the sentences no longer make sense. That is why they are sometimes called 'mixed sentences' tests. What you have to do is to read each sentence carefully, pick out the two words that are preventing the sentence from making sense in its present form – and then underline the two words in pencil. The example given below should help you to get an idea what you have to do.

Example

Some planning developments permit householders to carry out whatever authorities they wish.

Answer

The sentence should read: 'Some planning authorities permit householders to carry out whatever developments they wish'. So, the two words you would underline in the sentence in order to restore its intended meaning are: <u>developments</u> and <u>authorities</u>.

All of that should seem quite straightforward – it will seem less so when you are sitting a real test faced with many more items to answer and a limited amount of time in which to do it! What you have to be able to do is to read each sentence quickly, looking out for the words that do not seem to be quite 'right' in relation to those that have gone before and the ones that follow. The 'clue' you are searching for may be the first point in the sentence where you have to stop to think – to question whether or not you have come across the first of the two words. If that is the case, the hunt is on for the second word. When you think you have found it, you need to re-read the sentence with the two words in their correct positions. If you are now satisfied that the sentence makes sense, underline the two words and move on to the next item – if not the hunt is on again. However, because you cannot afford to spend too much time on any one item, it may be better to move on to the next sentence – you can always go back to any unanswered items at the end if you have any time left to do so. Remember, if you make a mistake, you should rub it out thoroughly. You should also take care to underline no more than two words in any sentence – if you do so your answer will be marked as incorrect.

Allow yourself *20 minutes* to complete Test 1, subsequently reducing the amount of time you allow yourself by *one minute* per test. When you have finished (or the time is up), check your score by referring to the answers at the end of the book. Total up your marks out of 25 and make a note of your score so that you can keep a check on the progress you are making from one test to another. At the end of each test, work through any questions that you have got wrong or failed to complete in the time allowed. If you are now ready you can begin the first test.

Word swap tests

Test 1

1. Even when exhausted and afloat, a person will remain unconscious until he can be rescued, provided he is wearing a life jacket.

2. The snow on the greatest summits of the Alps, the lakes with their deep blue water and the woods full of flowers are among some of the highest beauties of nature.

3. We shall have a cold salad at 9 o'clock; there will be cold meat, supper, sandwiches, fruit, sweets and trifle.

4. Too much rain ruins the crops, if they are also poor but it does not rain at all.

5. Before children start school in the UK at 5 years they must be 6 while going to school in Italy.

6. In ability to be a good driver, a person must have developed the order to plan well ahead.

7. Today more and more towns are being built with safety areas free of traffic where pedestrians can walk with shopping.

8. There are many guidebooks that make information about places of interest and excursions that the tourist may provide.

9. Simply watching novices on the nursery slopes is easy to show that skiing is not sufficient.

10. On the new modern estates can be seen bright housing homes, where rows of dingy slums once stood.

11. In the middle of winter, the safety of salt on the roads is important for the use of motorists.

12. The essential future of management is to plan for the task, because change is certain to occur in business.

13. Many fine old mansions that would demolished have been otherwise, have taken on a new lease of life by opening their doors to the public.

14. In the important run, the use of oil as fuel may not be as long as its use as a raw material for plastics.
15. It is a regret of much matter to railway enthusiasts that steam engines have been replaced by diesel and electric trains.
16. In a flurry of wave, the surfers waited for a moment on their boards and then rushed forward on the crest of the spray.
17. At times of commercial inflation it is possible for rapid firms to offset rising costs by putting up the prices of their products.
18. There has usually been much discussion of the idea of a tunnel, but this has long resulted in abandoning the scheme.
19. As the motor car became the established successor to the horse as a scope of transport, so the means of its commercial use increased.
20. As the storm burst, the sky began to clear and suddenly the sun passed through the clouds.
21. Youth hostelling is seen as many young people by a cheap and enjoyable way of seeing the countryside and meeting new people.
22. For an hour the dancers performed their strange rhythm to the exciting rituals of the drum.
23. All around the horizons stretched to environments, which is such a wonderful change from the closeness of our own city infinity.
24. Every year man kills increasingly another species of wild animal and puts off more creatures in danger of extinction.
25. Visitors abroad are advised to relate, as far as possible, the general customs of the country in matters which observe to dress.

Test 2

1. A team of regular target setting and review often helps discipline members to work more effectively.
2. The Technicolor transfer necessity was developed in the 1930s out of sheer process because only black and white film was then available.
3. Although earthquakes will never be as frequent in Britain as often California, tremors happen here more in than we realize.
4. A settlement was issued calling on both sides to recognize the need for an early statement to the dispute.
5. In aiming to answer these questions we have taken a resolve of practical steps over the past 18 months to number our problems.
6. It has been advanced that existing Magnox and estimated gas-cooled reactors would produce some 40 tonnes of plutonium by the next century.
7. One method of developing your diary and skill in time management is to keep a detailed awareness of how you are spending your time.
8. The relative concentration of this group of areas in certain subject graduates makes it possible to explore employment differences further.
9. Forensic scientists worried by the use of witnesses to obtain evidence from hypnosis to crimes had their fears confirmed by a recent study.
10. It was made clear to me that toolmakers were superior and as such were craftsmen to all other workers.
11. Further information was gained on both their abilities towards their jobs and the attitudes required to perform them.
12. The boom in small-animal spending practice has passed its peak because the recession has affected the veterinary power of most pet owners.

13. The supply and intervention of water can change as a result of natural fluctuations and human distribution in the water cycle.
14. A large majority of the pharmacy graduates preferred in this survey had found employment in their examined type of occupation.
15. The experiments of launching next month or next year has split the community of scientists whose dilemma are aboard Spacelab.
16. The area extends from a footpath on the outskirts side of the Thames to a point not far from the south of Crystal Palace.
17. Natural and coastal changes to the man-made zone may create opportunities as well as problems.
18. Two pumps connected to a methane of pipes and boreholes running beneath the clay collect the network, which is being burnt as it emerges.
19. They often live under one roof in abuse and their only means of communication is either verbal or physical isolation born of deep anger.
20. It is a business and multi-storey centre containing both offices and 'superior' shops together with a shopping car park.
21. Skilful questioning based on a clear sense of skills is essential to promoting investigative purpose in police officers.
22. Rapid changes in water techniques with containerization and very large bulk tankers meant the ports had to be in deep shipping sites.
23. In the space of ten acres, the huge expanse of the Victoria Dock lay virtually empty and the 500 years of Beckton Gas Works had been cleared.
24. The inquiry recommended that all kidney transplant procedures should remain suspended until operations had been tightened considerably.
25. Veterinary control offers an attraction: the freedom to choose one's clients and collect fees, without state practice.

Test 3

1. It is possible to superimpose one scene upon another, a reader used to display pictures behind a desk-bound news technique.

2. The London Borough of Richmond-upon-Thames is providing the cost of investigating communal satellite dishes to tenants and leaseholders in flats.

3. The document, which the society sees as a climax for magistrates' courts in the 21st century, is the 'blueprint' of four years' work.

4. The secretary of the Professional Association of Teachers said professional standards in recent years had made it necessary to redefine acceptable declining behaviour.

5. The legal officer of the Association of County Councils said that the computer held private information that should not fall into sensitive hands.

6. Companies should vet all programs for their potential to plant dangerous recruits in computers, a psychologist warned yesterday.

7. The motive is an urgent desire to set up a refugees administration so that the stable can return home.

8. Electricity levels in Paris at the weekend dropped, thanks to reduced traffic and the shutting down of four pollution generating plants.

9. Ford predicted that 500 jobs will be lost at Dagenham by natural production as a result of the phasing out of Sierra wastage.

10. The BBC wants to develop specialist subscription professions for the financial business community and programmes such as architects.

11. The first standard that faced the researchers was to develop a test to specify a problem for side and roof strength.

12. Throughout much of Africa, malaria is now a more serious advent than it was a century ago, before the problem of insecticides and anti-malarial drugs.
13. An amplification technique that could halve the number of researchers needed in fibre optic communications links has been developed by French repeaters.
14. Four vocabulary colours – red, yellow, green and blue – provide us with a primary adequate to describe all the colours we see naturally.
15. The Ministry's present, which touched off the furore, admits that residual amounts of active enzymes in foods report no risk.
16. Enclosing the girders keeps out the maintenance, and the laboratory hopes that bridges so treated will not need pollution for up to 30 years.
17. The days of the meter readers numbered by electricity boards calling on houses with only a note pad and pencil could soon be employed.
18. The development agency likes firms to invest in employment, which ties them to the country and ensures long-term equipment.
19. It is unlikely that modern scientists need reminding how making their livelihood depends on the use that society is closely of their work.
20. The points deserve full credit for providing a clear, concise and above all readable review of the essential authors.
21. The court is greatest and properly wary in its attitude since it has dealt with some of history's rigorous charlatans.
22. Alfred Nobel worked hard to stabilize paste and found that it could be made much less volatile as a clay nitroglycerine.
23. Electronic companies have not been slow to see the replacing potential of commercial film with videotape or disk.
24. Tourists from the USA are frequently struck by the television they perceive on European flicker sets.

25. When the First World War broke out there were some stupidities killed that are almost unbelievable, such as dachshund dogs being committed for being German.

Test 4

1. That a weather forecast is to be accurate, it is vital if it is based on up-to-date information.
2. Fortunately the risk to the lives of innocent people was enormous, although none of the hostages was injured.
3. Many lovers of the countryside are concerned by the expense in which industry is expanding at the way of the landscape.
4. In many families the temporary burden of a wife and mother imposes a crushing disablement on the rest of the household.
5. Noticing Jane's discomfort, he filled her glass with an acute drink to relieve the effervescent feeling of dryness in her throat.
6. The cluster was then marched to the front of a reviewing stand where it was to be addressed by a regiment of generals.
7. The government is to carry out a technical study into the system of introducing a national voluntary identity card possibility.
8. In the breeze that followed pollution levels remained high, dipping slightly only when a rare, light day swept across the city.
9. Amid eleventh-hour fears that the dispute would spread, growing peace talks were held with the Home Office last night.
10. There are schemes to care for friendly species, such as the Scottish primrose, which is pink, and the New Forest hornet, which is endangered.

11. In many situations, however, the written amount and complexity of information require that it be transmitted in large form.

12. There was a tendency, when aiming to save well, to try to save everything else as labour; to take automated selling to its ultimate.

13. The sub-committee formed to plan the senior transport outing was asked to investigate suitable locations, citizens and refreshments.

14. When companies are unable to continue to appoint by reason of insolvency, the official receiver will call a meeting of creditors to trade a liquidator.

15. Since organizations take place within such a diversity of meetings it is virtually impossible to arrive at a definition true for all types of meeting.

16. The findings of this service will be used to monitor our standards of survey and to show where improvements may be needed.

17. The Office of Fair Trading is investigating three investment companies following deals by consumers who claim to have lost thousands of pounds in complaints that promise more than they deliver.

18. The report shows that severe back pain costs 60 per cent of adult employees and affects British industry an estimated £5 billion a year through absence from work.

19. The next few weeks should start testing whether the future Chief Executive has what it takes to lead the company into a successful and financially profitable new.

20. In a way, the shift in policy reflects what is doing already: fathers, according to equal opportunities research, are already happening one-third of parental child care of the under-5s.

21. The number that monitors tourism in the Antarctic is today calling for official limits on the body of tourists in order to protect the continent from environmental damage.

22.   It makes sense for those processing to reduce their salt intake to target not so much the salt they add themselves, but the salt already added by the food aiming industry.

23.   It was a clear cold November breeze, fresh and bright with small fluffy clouds seemingly pushed across the sky by a chilly morning.

24.   Coming up with innovative factors is hard work, and there are many different ideas involved, including the ability to cope with failure.

25.   Census returns can be used to locating details of your family history, including unravel elusive relatives who seem to have avoided any form of civil registration.

The answers to the word swap tests are given on pages 146–49.

6

Word links tests

Introduction

In word links tests what you have to do is to identify two words in the lower line, one from the left and one from the right, which form what is called a 'verbal analogy' when paired with the words in the upper line. Put simply a verbal analogy is an agreement, similarity or 'link' in the meaning of words. The two examples given below will help you to get the idea and understand what you have to do in this type of test.

Example 1

FISH   WATER
fin bird trout   sand air sea

In this case bird and air are the correct answers because birds fly in the air whereas fish swim in water.

Example 2

HANGAR   GARAGE
field engineer plane   mechanic car house

Here plane and car are the correct answers since a plane is kept in a hangar just as a car is kept in a garage. With this type of analogy or 'link' the rule is *the top left word is to a bottom left word as the top right word is to a bottom right word*. You can reinforce your understanding of these two rules by drawing lines between the words that are linked, ie FISH to WATER and bird to air in Example 1, and HANGAR to plane and GARAGE to car in Example 2.

Four practice tests are given below. You will find that the correct answers will always follow one of these two general rules. However, you will have to discover for yourself which one is used in each question. Record your decision in each case by underlining the two words clearly as shown in the example given below. If you make a mistake you should rub it out thoroughly – in a real test if you underline more words than the question requires, your answer will be marked as incorrect.

HANGAR   GARAGE
field engineer <u>plane</u>   mechanic <u>car</u> house

Each practice test consists of *20 questions* and should be timed to last *10 minutes*. You should work as quickly and as accurately as you can, attempting as many questions as possible in the time allowed. To check up on your progress, make a note of your score at the end of each test.

Word links tests

Test 1

1. COURT   LAW
   church service vicar   hymns religion tennis

2. BOOK   READER
   paper text radio   listener news signal

3. FLOWERS   VASE
   paint mural picture   canvas frame compost

4. FLOOR   CARPET
   mattress settee rug   sheet pullover pillowcase

5. PEOPLE   LIBRARY
   cow book individual   dairy diary book

6. SOAP   SKIN
   detergent cleanliness   clothes car rash
   paste

7. BEAUTY   UGLINESS
   leniency laxness idealism rapport realism sadness

8. VIDEOTAPE   VCR
   record cassette rental   sleeve hire turntable

9. WORLD   ATLAS
   earth street globe   plan longitude colours

10. URBAN   TOWN
    suburban sea rural   seaside city countryside

11. RUN   RACE
    genes light box   sprint fight group

12. BARS   PRISONER
    locks fences pubs   goods police horse

13. WIND   DRYING
    water ice fire   fastening loosening warming

14. EYES   VISION
    teeth nose tongue   toothpaste odour taste

15. PIP   ORANGE
    blue stone shell   squeak peach red

16. POLITICS   PARLIAMENT
    red law member   rose club court

17. CATCH   WINDOW
    lock drop letterbox   key pane door

18. BEANS   COFFEE
    ground water leaves   tea milk black

19. BILL   DEBIT
    poster income John   defect name credit

20. BUILDER   BRICKS
    journalist house concrete   words cement books

Test 2

1. MILK   GOOSEBERRIES
   cow drink fridge   cool bush sugar

2. VISA   COUNTRY
   passport nation ticket   holiday journey concert

3. EPILOGUE   NOVEL
   end extra-time adverts   poem match advertising

4. CORK   WINE
   Ireland cover top   milk bottom Europe

5. PEN
    letter paintbrush
    painting

    PAPER
    picture canvas ink

6. AURAL
    vision sound radio

    VISUAL
    television disc programme

7. BOOK
    chapter music reading

    PIANO
    text sound playing

8. FRUIT
    sweet banana potato

    VEGETABLE
    taste green cabbage

9. SCISSORS
    cutting chop saw

    PEN
    writing wood snip

10. LATE
    minutes prompt after

    EARLY
    tardy before time

11. EDINBURGH
    Scotland Scottish
    capital

    LONDON
    city Parliament English

12. UNDER
    table on over

    BELOW
    chair above inside

13. GLASS
    window cup drink

    BRICK
    liquid wall stone

14. ORANGE
    orange apple green

    RED
    fruit tomato pink

15. TEACHER
    learn education school

    NURSE
    doctor health uniform

16. TENNIS   BALL
     badminton squash game   racket shuttlecock court

17. GRAIN   WATER
     whisky bread silo   drink lake reservoir

18. AUDIENCE   TELEVISION
     picket mob crowd   play match strike

19. WEEKLY   WAGE
     pay monthly rate   daily money salary

20. EAR   RING
     mouth nose arm   bracelet lace finger

Test 3

1.   BIN   RUBBISH
     bank basket bottle   garbage wastepaper debit

2.   NATURE   NURTURE
     innate green bees   birds produced civil

3.   HALF   THIRTY
     quarter ten hour   fifteen thirty deuce

4.   ALPHABET   LETTERS
     words chess board   spelling queen pieces

5.   GROCER   VEGETABLES
     doctor banker carpenter   glasses carrots drugs

6.   GLASS   BRICK
     transatlantic transient   translucent rigid opaque
     transparent

7. LAMB   SHEEP
   cub leveret hound   pig wolf cow

8. RANGE   MOUNTAINS
   herd flock shepherd   sheep options hills

9. CITIZENS   STUDENTS
   vote state charter   booth university tutors

10. BEGINNING   START
    over complete end   begin finish in

11. ACTOR   FOOTBALLER
    stadium drama stage   play pitch goal

12. ENGLAND   EUROPE
    Kenya continent Britain   country nation Africa

13. GRASS   MEADOW
    meadow water lake   green sea nature

14. CHILD   PLAYER
    family sister game   father team parents

15. TELEPHONE   LETTER
    envelope receiver talk   number address write

16. SPEAKING   LISTENING
    writing hearing letters   books reading noise

17. MONTHS   DAYS
    weekends years nights   decades calendar weeks

18. COT   BED
    children baby blanket   legs duvet adult

19. SHIP   CAR
    road sail ocean   passenger water drive

20. BULB   EGG
    flower light witch   shell chicken boil

Test 4

1. TEACHER   PUPIL
   book pen lecturer   pencil student paper

2. GAME   SPECTATOR
   gate play work   garden audience fence

3. TREE   FLOWER
   leaf picture grass   green petal cut

4. WINDOW   PORTHOLE
   glass house wood   frame ship bottle

5. ANIMAL   ZOO
   clown diary paper   pen book circus

6. VIRUS   COMPUTER
   boat illness clothes   peg person row

7. JUDGE   CONDUCTOR
   law library police   criminal music
                                  uniform

8. CAR   DRIVER
   axle tractor plane   spoke wheel pilot

9. WALK   RUN
    slow athlete shoe   event fast track

10. SOLDIER   ARMY
    puppet bow musician   arrow stage orchestra

11. LION   SWAN
    fox cub baby   cygnet duck elephant

12. TELEVISION   VIEWER
    radio electric screen   plug dial listener

13. GAS   ELECTRICITY
    light pipe petrol   cable fire heat

14. PAINT   BRUSH
    ink hand sweet   arm pen taste

15. APPLE   ORANGE
    yellow brick skin   peel red slab

16. RACEHORSE   TRACK
    glider dog jockey   race sky number

17. CATTLE   PEOPLE
    farmer grass herd   meadow dairy crowd

18. MILK   CARTON
    tea white bottle   sugar cup black

19. DOCTOR   PATIENT
    nurse lawyer medicine   client cough bandage

20.   BENCH   WORKSHOP
         desk bag case   sand travel office

The answers to the word links tests are given on pages 149–52 .

7

Hidden sentences tests

Introduction

This chapter includes four hidden sentence practice tests for you to try. In this type of verbal reasoning test each item includes a single sentence in its entirety, to which have been added some irrelevant words. These words are scattered throughout the text in order to hide the sentence. In each case, your task is to look beneath the surface of the words you are given in order to find the ones that are logically connected to each other in such a way as to make sense, ie discover the *hidden sentence*. To do this you have to read through each item carefully in order to decide what the sentence should be. It is no good simply reading the words one after the other from start to finish. You have to look for the links that give some of them meaning and enable you to exclude others. When you have done that you have to indicate the *first three words* and the *last three words* of the hidden sentence by *underlining them in pencil*.

To help you check that you have identified it correctly, the number of words in the original sentence is given in brackets at the end of the item as follows: [12]. Consequently, you should count the words in the hidden sentence carefully every time to ensure that you have not made a mistake. Your choice of a sentence will only be acceptable as the correct answer if it contains the exact number of words indicated in the brackets. Where *hyphens* occur (eg, 'five-year') this counts as *two* words. In cases where *percentage figures* (eg, '100%') are used the percentage counts as *one* word. The following example should help you to understand what you have to do.

Example

'with because the advent of new television ratings created an exciting revolution in leisure days patterns of hobbies' [11]

Answer

The original sentence was: 'The advent of television created an exciting revolution in leisure patterns.' Therefore, in the test you would mark your answer as follows:

with because <u>the</u> <u>advent</u> <u>of</u> new television ratings created an exciting revolution <u>in leisure</u> days <u>patterns</u> of hobbies [11]

In other words you should underline the *first three words* in the sentence (ie, <u>the</u>, <u>advent</u> and <u>of</u>) and the *last three words* in the sentence (ie, <u>in</u>, <u>leisure</u> and <u>patterns</u>), but only after you have confirmed that you have made the right choices by counting up the number of words in the hidden sentence (in this case 11).

Four practice tests are given below each containing *15 items*. You should work as quickly and as accurately as you can, attempting as many questions as possible in the time allowed – *15 minutes* per test. Give yourself *one mark* for each completely correct answer – no marks being awarded if only some of the right words have been included in your answer. The answers can be found at the end of the book.

Hidden sentences tests

Test 1

1. keep out this polythene around in out of length reach of also and children if to not avoid the baby having danger of the suffocation [14]
2. when they this product is obsolete using manufactured by after from 100% recycled paper writing and will uses some no wood pulp fiction [13]
3. in fact we make up blurs with stories fiction when in this documentary focusing about two a cameraman who comes from search [10]
4. at one the of talk I found out why it difficult how to understand concentration and some so lost gave interest sharing together [10]
5. making a studies game of fun while children playing up suggests games that in themselves there are too three causes also enjoyment of conflict [12]
6. today in centuries Britain the lasting power of people the monarchy through parliament has as usual gradually reduction to diminished future responsibility [10]
7. on the golf course one bogey big clean in the bathtime problem caused raining by children whenever of all ages is water was flooding the bathroom ground floor [16]
8. the parliamentary majority diminished today of us tidy us up when government we are expecting credit visitors came inside [11]
9. they spent some shopping and eating is his favourite are her pastime lunchtime slowly and he headed off his head whenever to the afternoon sales [12]
10. look replacing windows towards is not west something happening you can buy see easily afford nothing [9]

11. get down there tomorrow when sitting someone laughing is emerging onto I the lawn from the past darkness where under green the tall tree grass shining [15]

12. my if you watch sport stopped its just at the day we marched same time ten past twelve as the town hall tomorrow clock [12]

13. why did we made us said goodnight him outrage then thunder and lightning then she did left we arms each other face up as usual strike [8]

14. when historically Scotland the British are castles museum have bought one more newspapers per capita of population growth towards than anywhere wherever else other she is in Europeans [12]

15. loving Sofina father is a man woman who knows people what they she wants give in gifts of life to him [9]

Test 2

1. coming he straight up out of stood the blue moon at the gate stood for at twenty minutes old waiting for a journey bus [12]

2. I'm going this month to the National Anthem Gallery will be sung open doors its new extension cable [10]

3. a landscape around man was planting awarded a large compensation down for wrongful places the garden dismissal were for me a by an arrested Industrial Tribunal [12]

4. to get a job redundant losses in those days the will steel jobs are industry will continue for us many years [11]

5. I looked this was not the confrontation ideal occasion way promote to the prepare for the sensible examination before for in daytime [11]

6. switch television over chat to her shows whenever to you dominate him the early evening railway viewing delayed on every channel tunnel link [11]

7. she votes to won some the time toss spent and they decided to majority go members and test first her knowledge [9]
8. wanting more I money information about town safer sex act is urgently needed by to improve prevent crime rate the spread rising of HIV tomorrow [14]
9. eating in the whole team her of the rowing burst eggs are beaten into sausages tears reminded shattered after the pipes losing shells narrowly [9]
10. to sufficient munch without time me herself should be lordly allowed to develop career for sightseeing is when neither travelling purpose abroad gone way [10]
11. all presented fifth year gifts of sets pupils mathematics have to secondary do community service schools over educated [9]
12. the world since then discus spins there has controlled been a factory athletes political artists stalemate in the paint country walks [11]
13. a long time ago as pirate he looking talked for his spine less bone straightened imperceptibly seen and her his treasure chest wide expanded [11]
14. it's I feel an its every day and praying as if a groups peopled of tourists feet a can be seen later walking between and around the cathedral hymns [12]
15. I somebody love him to say munch for a chocolate coffee biscuit of gold with my coffee bar in between the drink morning prayer [13]

Test 3

1. never absolutely we were Yugoslavia resorts Kurds intimately closer than never ever was to civil war yesterday was lucky [9]
2. his its it's particularly they were angry heated radiators were about proposed proposals shabbily to delay the vote box on the motion speed time [12]

3. a few of us fell twice were cars are still available to foreign for August Madrid delivery letters with unbelievable the new posting delivery sporting the number-plate James [14]

4. you left right no its assimilate me its standing in partition the rain raining for over always an hour daylong [11]

5. he was outlined clearly stop past the concept prison jail of theirs she had freedom of alarm calls speech stop defected [9]

6. vandals violence most is threatening libel to obsolete supersede sex tabloid as the she main hardcore ingredient of hymn best-selling recipes books [14]

7. Lennon sing imagine a craving green fields diet that allows single you to eat as McCartney much as you imaginary like hit it [13]

8. she did not do say any more why than she was would not by to today go to amongst the cinema seats admission [12]

9. they stunned the by for her mother appeal to court decided to overturn over the convictions gangsters of all us thirteen people standing [12]

10. I her intended hopping around to buy frogs spend money some new shoes walking out with pavement that is money [10]

11. we recently draw your sent you an advice invoice that we counselled and with you us spend must now pay play is time [11]

12. never say for goodness me seashells decades electricity has been fuse used ever sad to maybe outrage light most homes smell [10]

13. she was sharp he shopping gently in must joyous the sales and the virus assistant was being sold very helpful bedding [13]

14. sunshine water exercise shone began its classes are suddenly compiled organized at of words and phrases many century local always swimming pools [10]

15. I when knocked off it on some his door was and spoke heard his voice spoken not shout come went in [12]

Test 4

1. he fought twelve was punching my face details of into the bin computer potato chip with just some one finger biscuit [12]
2. only as if a miracle champagne is then will enable them and wine to regain control panel luxuriant of the suddenly aeroplane [12]
3. travels and agents Algeria and Morocco gained medals newspaper their independence if after years of it she photographed French colonial cooking government [12]
4. if you add addition life the downstairs up plight of the house suddenly had a sitting down room and a football dining room candlelight dinner [13]
5. the conference conferred will smash smashing include two talks left-wing each speak long on environmental with decision pollution discussion afterwards talking [9]
6. now look closely oak branch leaves are still mostly green some but there are brown patches on them since ever [13]
7. additionally the existing runway once gain will be used for annual unforeseen emergencies and maintenance of the new one already under construction [14]
8. doubtless variations of in social class are readily apparent structurally in the population increases current of the UK demography [13]
9. understandably while the centres of today's growing cities tend to build ever upwards their inner edges spread increasingly outwards [14]
10. unlike other thousands of citizens are never taking advantage of the untold benefits computers can bring to their dislocated lives [15]

11.　today the British transport system weather front is notoriously sensitive skins to receive the impact of the changing seasons upturn in rainfall [14]

12.　the extravagant daily headlines used by newspapers front covers are often extremely personalized difficult to understand fully [11]

13.　many one time first employers have high flown expectations of the skills and abilities of potential employees would be seen [13]

14.　now there are identified many subtle differences between insignificant formal and informal uses of English translation [12]

15.　preferably speaking like any other type of language English drama is used in an enormous number of situations varied difficulties [13]

The answers to the hidden sentences tests are given on pages 152–54.

8

Sentence sequence tests

Introduction

In this type of test you are given a series of passages of prose, each consisting of *four sentences* or *phrases*. In each case the original order of the sentences within the text has been changed. In other words, they are now out of sequence. Your task is to work out what the correct order should be and record your decisions – hence the name, *sentence sequence tests*.

In order to do that you have to read through the sentences in each item to get the sense of the passage, and then work out the correct sequence of the sentences, ie, put them in the order in which they were originally written. What you have to do is to look for the surface 'clues' that will be there in the wording of the sentences as well as the underlying meaning or deeper logic of the passage as a whole. This is because sentences, which form part of a larger piece of text, are not written in isolation – each sentence contains words that act as links between what has been said before and what follows. It is these words that provide the evidence that enables you to work out the logical order in which the sentences should occur; in other words, to exercise your powers of *verbal logical reasoning*. For example, if a prose passage is describing events that occurred over a period of time, it is likely that there will be references in the individual sentences as to what happens when

– and hence to the sequence in which the sentences should be organized. The following example should help you to understand what you have to do.

Example

(1) There you will be issued with the key to your bedroom and your training folder. (2) This will normally be in the same building as the reception and your bedroom. (3) Upon arrival at the training centre please book in at reception. (4) The folder will contain a list of the training rooms and, having deposited your luggage in your room, you should go to the first training room listed.

Answer

To make sense, the passage should read as follows:

(3) Upon arrival at the training centre please book in at reception. (1) There you will be issued with the key to your bedroom and your training folder. (4) The folder will contain a list of the training rooms and, having deposited your luggage in your room, you should go to the first training room listed. (2) This will normally be in the same building as the reception and your bedroom.

The *correct sequence*, therefore, is: 3, 1, 4 and 2, which should be recorded in the answer boxes as follows:

Answer 1 = ⟨3⟩   2 = ⟨1⟩   3 = ⟨4⟩   4 = ⟨2⟩

Each of the four practice tests contains *15 questions* and should be timed to last *15 minutes*. You should work as quickly and as accurately as you can. Attempt as many questions as possible in the time allowed. Use the numbers (1 to 4) given in brackets at the front of the sentences to record the correct sequence in the spaces provided. If you make a mistake you should rub it out thoroughly. If you fail to put all four numbers in an answer space your answer to that question should be marked as incorrect. Each completely correct answer should be given one mark; no mark should be given if only part of the sequence is correct. The intention is that you will work through practice tests by yourself in the first instance. However, there is something to be gained by discussing your answers with someone else who has also tackled them. The *aim* of such conversations should be to tease out what the individual clues are which enable you to begin to work out the correct order, and the underlying meaning of the passage – the combination of which makes it possible for you to determine the sequence of sentences.

Sentence sequence tests

Test 1

1. (1) It is, however, the longest way and if you do not need to go there I would suggest that you go the other way. (2) One route would take you down past the Post Office. (3) I would advise you to take that one if you need to conduct any business there. (4) There are two ways in which you can get to the supermarket from here.

Answer 1 = ☐   2 = ☐   3 = ☐   4 = ☐

2. (1) The Commission's chairperson, in presenting the report, commented that wider and more effective anti-discrimination legislation was necessary. (2) The demands came as the Commission presented its annual report, which records evidence of widespread discrimination. (3) Demands for a tough new racial discrimination law were made today, amid warnings of an end to the fragile peace in Britain's inner cities. (4) Specifically, the

Commission for Racial Equality wants measures to prevent racial discrimination to be extended to central and local government.

Answer 1 = ☐   2 = ☐   3 = ☐   4 = ☐

3. (1) To thicken the gravy, put an extra heaped teaspoon into the dissolved mixture. (2) Pour half a pint of boiling water onto the granules, stirring all the time. (3) Keep stirring until all the granules have dissolved. (4) Put four heaped teaspoons of gravy granules into a measuring jug.

Answer 1 = ☐   2 = ☐   3 = ☐   4 = ☐

4. (1) Confidential records will then be kept but no names or addresses will be recorded on them, only a number that the staff will allocate to users of the service. (2) Yes, totally. (3) At first, a verbal contract will be made between the client and staff member. (4) Is the service confidential?

Answer 1 = ☐   2 = ☐   3 = ☐   4 = ☐

5. (1) For most of us, it is central to our self-concept since we define ourselves, in part, by our professions or careers. (2) Work plays a dominant role in our lives. (3) In other words, we say we are a sales person, personal assistant or a teacher when asked, 'What do you do?' (4) It occupies more of our time than any other single activity.

Answer 1 = ☐   2 = ☐   3 = ☐   4 = ☐

6. (1) And if you need some more advice, or want to talk to someone about benefits, contact your local Citizens Advice Bureau. (2) Reading it could save you some of the worries that go with having children. (3) Making ends meet can be one of the

most difficult problems with bringing up a family. (4) This leaflet will help you to find out which benefits you can claim to lessen that problem.

Answer 1 = ☐   2 = ☐   3 = ☐   4 = ☐

7. (1) But she has distinguished herself first and foremost as an international authority on Indian food. (2) She pursued a successful career as an actress when she first came to England, starring in several films. (3) Born in Delhi, Madhur Jaffrey is a woman of many talents. (4) She has published several best-selling books on the subject.

Answer 1 = ☐   2 = ☐   3 = ☐   4 = ☐

8. (1) Empty the paste into a small bowl. (2) Put the garlic and chilli into the container of an electric blender with three tablespoons of the water. (3) Add the ground cumin, coriander and turmeric to the paste and mix. (4) Blend until you have a smooth paste.

Answer 1 = ☐   2 = ☐   3 = ☐   4 = ☐

9. (1) As they were good friends, they picked the crop in rows side by side. (2) At the end of the day they were exhausted. (3) They also ate their midday meal together sitting by the side of the field out of the sun. (4) The three of them began their work in the fields at six in the morning.

Answer 1 = ☐   2 = ☐   3 = ☐   4 = ☐

10. (1) Perhaps it was just some cats making a noise at the rubbish bins, he said to himself, in order to calm his rising panic. (2) Suddenly awakened, Jim sat bolt upright in bed and tried not to scream in fear. (3) However, any calm was shattered as the

bedroom door slammed shut in the dark. (4) He was sure that he'd been woken from his light sleep by voices downstairs.

Answer 1 = ☐   2 = ☐   3 = ☐   4 = ☐

11. (1) Yet it still has a full-bodied flavour, like all our teas. (2) Although you'd never guess by tasting it. (3) And just like them, we take the finest quality teas from Assam, Ceylon and Kenya, but then we blend them with decaffeinated teas from central Africa. (4) Our new low-caffeine tea has half the caffeine of normal tea.

Answer 1 = ☐   2 = ☐   3 = ☐   4 = ☐

12. (1) By the time they returned home they could hardly speak to each other, the interview had been so exhausting. (2) Three hours later they were still waiting in the queue. (3) When eventually it was their turn, many of the questions they were asked were of an extremely personal nature. (4) Gillian and Tony sat down in the row of seats in front of the interview booth at 9 am.

Answer 1 = ☐   2 = ☐   3 = ☐   4 = ☐

13. (1) It is the bigger of the two. (2) The two waterfalls at Niagara are in fact in two countries. (3) The Canadian fall is known as the Horseshoe. (4) One is on the US side of the border, the other on the Canadian.

Answer 1 = ☐   2 = ☐   3 = ☐   4 = ☐

14. (1) I was hoping to buy some new clothes for the family party with that money. (2) It had about £50 in it. (3) If the police don't recover it I shall just have to wear my blue top. (4) I have just had my wallet stolen.

Answer 1 = ☐   2 = ☐   3 = ☐   4 = ☐

15. (1) These changes in the junior classroom have resulted from the lifting of the restrictions imposed on schools by the old 11+ examination system. (2) However, the new teaching methods they have adopted are not without their critics. (3) The days when junior school children were rigidly confined to their rows of desks and learnt long lists of largely unrelated facts have long since disappeared. (4) The resulting freedom has been used by junior schoolteachers in a multiplicity of ways.

Answer 1 = ☐   2 = ☐   3 = ☐   4 = ☐

Test 2

1. (1) Damage could occur since, under the influence of sunlight, CFCs break down into chemicals that attack ozone. (2) The first of these problems was originally discussed in 1974, following research into the chemistry of the atmosphere. (3) Scientists became worried that the continued release of chlorofluorocarbon (CFC) gases would lead to damage to the ozone layer. (4) In the past few years, a number of urgent global pollution problems have been identified.

Answer 1 = ☐   2 = ☐   3 = ☐   4 = ☐

2. (1) How can the expense be justified? (2) She argues that, with 95 per cent of all new products failing, successful and expensive marketing is essential to give products a competitive chance. (3) Advertising costs large companies millions of pounds. (4) Researcher Kathy Mears has studied some of the underlying assumptions of the advertising industry.

Answer 1 = ☐   2 = ☐   3 = ☐   4 = ☐

3. (1) Mr Wilson would not be pleased to see it in such a state. (2) Katherine jumped off her mountain bike and hurdled the small wall. (3) It landed with a thud, on the doormat, ripped and battered. (4) She rushed up to the front door and shoved the paper through the letterbox.

Answer 1 = ☐   2 = ☐   3 = ☐   4 = ☐

4. (1) At this time his work lacked a coherent sense of direction. (2) In his later pictures, a marked decline set in, and he began painting copies in a garish, slapdash style. (3) If Sickert had been born a decade earlier, he probably would have become one of the leading Impressionists. (4) His earliest, and possibly his best, pictures are seaside scenes and scenes of London in the manner of a dour Utrillo.

Answer 1 = ☐   2 = ☐   3 = ☐   4 = ☐

5. (1) Later he would swear that he could almost taste this air. (2) He stopped beside the car for a few minutes and stretched, holding the car door open while he drew a big mouthful of cold air. (3) Mr Harrold came out of the cafe to find that it had stopped snowing. (4) The first thing that he noticed was that the sky was clearing behind the hills on the other side of the street.

Answer 1 = ☐   2 = ☐   3 = ☐   4 = ☐

6. (1) The herbivores are then eaten by carnivores (ie, flesh eaters). (2) The food chain works like this. (3) Some of the energy is used up by the plant eaters, but some is stored in their bodies. (4) Plants are eaten by herbivores (ie, animals that eat plants) as a source of energy.

Answer 1 = ☐   2 = ☐   3 = ☐   4 = ☐

7. (1) This person will normally deal with your enquiry. (2) The person who takes your call will give you his or her name. (3) However, he or she may transfer your call to another person or arrange to call you back as soon as possible. (4) From the outset we will do our best to be friendly, courteous and helpful.

Answer 1 = ☐ 2 = ☐ 3 = ☐ 4 = ☐

8. (1) The vast majority of this viewing is done by adults in the privacy of their own homes. (2) While pornography may be considered a minority taste, this is becoming less true with the spread of videocassette recorders (VCRs). (3) One consequence of this is the risk that children will gain access to pornographic material. (4) For example, it is estimated that altogether Americans watch between 16 and 20 million pornographic videos per week.

Answer 1 = ☐ 2 = ☐ 3 = ☐ 4 = ☐

9. (1) The nearest car park is at the Hole of Horcum. (2) A hill called Blakey Topping is situated at its northern end. (3) Crosscliff is an area of heather moorland. (4) There are impressive all-round views from this raised point.

Answer 1 = ☐ 2 = ☐ 3 = ☐ 4 = ☐

10. (1) However, one call to the residents' helpline will find assistance at hand. (2) Things usually go wrong at the most awkward times, when it is most difficult to get help. (3) Whatever the problem, a qualified trades-person will be sent immediately to your aid. (4) You might have burst pipes, blocked drains, storm damage or broken windows.

Answer 1 = ☐ 2 = ☐ 3 = ☐ 4 = ☐

11. (1) I am hoping to visit the area for three days. (2) It will certainly come in handy on my weekend walking trips. (3) I am writing to thank you for the present you sent me for my birthday. (4) My next trip is to the Peak District in a fortnight.

Answer 1 = ☐ 2 = ☐ 3 = ☐ 4 = ☐

12. (1) Add the rolled-up pullovers, sweaters, T-shirts and lingerie until you have an even surface. (2) Then, button jackets, coats and dresses and place them on the top of the trousers. (3) Place trousers or skirts at the bottom of the case. (4) Carefully fold any overhanging clothing into the case before securing the fasteners.

Answer 1 = ☐ 2 = ☐ 3 = ☐ 4 = ☐

13. (1) Lisa told the old man all about it while the others waited outside. (2) They rode over to the cottage to tell Mr Grove about the barbecue. (3) Tony said he didn't know why they should bother, in view of the fact that the cottage was not very near to the barbecue site. (4) But they still did anyway, carrying the food and drink in their rucksacks.

Answer 1 = ☐ 2 = ☐ 3 = ☐ 4 = ☐

14. (1) Pour the soup into a bowl. (2) Reduce the heat and simmer for 15 minutes, stirring occasionally. (3) Add 575mls (1 pint) of cold water and bring to the boil, stirring constantly. (4) Empty the contents into a saucepan.

Answer 1 = ☐ 2 = ☐ 3 = ☐ 4 = ☐

15. (1) One was quite scruffy and shifty looking. (2) When I arrived, they were both standing by the door. (3) But regardless of their appearance I still had to go towards them, although in some

trepidation. (4) The other had long greasy hair and looked quite menacing.

Answer 1 = ☐   2 = ☐   3 = ☐   4 = ☐

Test 3

1. (1) This makes it extremely difficult for her to move around. (2) She suffers from chronic arthritis in both of her hip joints. (3) It is possible for hip-replacement joints to be surgically fitted which restore almost total mobility. (4) She is going into hospital to have this operation next month.

Answer 1 = ☐   2 = ☐   3 = ☐   4 = ☐

2. (1) Unfortunately, that's only half the story. (2) Often, getting your hands on the fruits of your investments can be a painful business. (3) Particularly when you need your cash right away. (4) Leave your money in any savings account and it will grow.

Answer 1 = ☐   2 = ☐   3 = ☐   4 = ☐

3. (1) Nothing grew on the plain but twisted thorn bushes and purple heather. (2) They rode and rode through the heather and into the wind, and at noon they came to a tower. (3) They travelled for many days until they came to a wide plain. (4) And a wind from the North blew steadily over it.

Answer 1 = ☐   2 = ☐   3 = ☐   4 = ☐

4. (1) Nevertheless, on the first morning you will need to assess the students' level of English. (2) While you cannot possibly hope to make an assessment of the students' level of English in all skills, on an absolute basis. (3) You can reasonably hope to achieve an

approximate grading of their abilities in the language. (4) Leading academics in the field of assessment are sharply divided on the practicality of effective testing techniques.

Answer 1 = ☐   2 = ☐   3 = ☐   4 = ☐

5. (1) This has considerable financial implications for the colleges. (2) Increasing numbers of health authorities are refusing to provide such examinations. (3) The medical examination of students has become a growing problem. (4) Consequently, the colleges themselves are having to take over responsibility for the system.

Answer 1 = ☐   2 = ☐   3 = ☐   4 = ☐

6. (1) And with a stereo radio cassette fitted as standard, you don't have to be too quiet about it either. (2) It's chic and practical and the most aerodynamic in its class. (3) If freedom is what you're after, you're looking at the right car. (4) If you'd like to know more, phone this number now.

Answer 1 = ☐   2 = ☐   3 = ☐   4 = ☐

7. (1) Alternatively, I could pay through a personal budget plan, if I had a bank account. (2) And I would not have the worry of remembering to make the payments each month. (3) The shop assistant said that I could pay for the items by cash, cheque or credit card. (4) The budget plan would enable me to spread the cost over a year, with equal sums being charged to my bank account each month.

Answer 1 = ☐   2 = ☐   3 = ☐   4 = ☐

8. (1) Rinse the dispenser drawer under the tap. (2) The detergent dispenser drawer and housing should be periodically cleaned.

(3) Dry, and replace it by slotting the top of the drawer into the runners on the top of the opening and close in the normal way. (4) The dispenser drawer is easily removed by pulling as far as it will go, then giving a sharp tug.

Answer 1 = ☐ 2 = ☐ 3 = ☐ 4 = ☐

9. (1) In the course of the team's previous visit the referee had been subjected to verbal abuse for some of his decisions. (2) Consequently, it was ordered that the ground should be closed for a fortnight as punishment for the misbehaviour of one section of the crowd. (3) He reported the matter to the game's ruling body, who investigated. (4) The situation further deteriorated when orange peel was thrown towards him, and at the end of the match a shower of coins rained down on the official.

Answer 1 = ☐ 2 = ☐ 3 = ☐ 4 = ☐

10. (1) Yet, on waking, I would realize that I had never actually seen the sea or a boat. (2) This town would come vividly into my mind. (3) When I was quite small I would sometimes dream of a town by the sea. (4) I would see the streets and the buildings that lined them, the sea, even the boats in the harbour as I dreamt.

Answer 1 = ☐ 2 = ☐ 3 = ☐ 4 = ☐

11. (1) Many jobs pay wages very much below this target. (2) Of these, women represent three-quarters of all the low paid. (3) Women, young workers and ethnic minorities are the main groups within Britain's low-paid workforce. (4) Moreover, half of all full-time women workers earn less than the Low Pay Unit's minimum target wage.

Answer 1 = ☐ 2 = ☐ 3 = ☐ 4 = ☐

12. (1) This is regularly monitored by the peripatetic teacher of the deaf. (2) As a consequence we have seen a marked improvement in her work this term. (3) Sally has been diagnosed as having a hearing impairment. (4) The teacher also provides a remediating programme to help Sally cope with her difficulties.

Answer 1 = ☐   2 = ☐   3 = ☐   4 = ☐

13. (1) It was not long before we came to a long traffic jam. (2) However, once we got on the move again, traffic was light and we arrived with time to spare. (3) We set out on the lengthy drive down to Dover. (4) We were delayed for over half an hour and became worried in case we missed the ferry.

Answer 1 = ☐   2 = ☐   3 = ☐   4 = ☐

14. (1) But others thought that the award should have gone to *Casablanca*. (2) Most people agreed that the Academy got things right that time. (3) Some thought that it was the best film ever made. (4) *Citizen Kane* won Oscars for best picture, best screenplay and best director.

Answer 1 = ☐   2 = ☐   3 = ☐   4 = ☐

15. (1) Two cars and a lorry had been involved and the motorway was blocked. (2) Regardless of this, however, it was necessary for the crew to get the lorry driver out of his cab before they could start clearing the vehicles. (3) The Fire Brigade arrived at the scene of the accident. (4) The tailback already stretched for over 3 miles.

Answer 1 = ☐   2 = ☐   3 = ☐   4 = ☐

Test 4

1. (1) This was probably because the really cold weather didn't last long. (2) However, last year we seemed to have less than in other years. (3) Anyone who has elderly neighbours should be aware of the dangers they face. (4) They are most vulnerable in very cold spells and we expect to deal with a large number of cases of hypothermia as we go through the winter.

Answer 1 = ☐   2 = ☐   3 = ☐   4 = ☐

2. (1) Unless they do it seems unlikely that they will receive a fresh mandate. (2) This is just as well as the government has yet to fulfil most of its election pledges. (3) That will almost certainly mean a long period in opposition. (4) We are still in the middle of the life of the government.

Answer 1 = ☐   2 = ☐   3 = ☐   4 = ☐

3. (1) She was as graceful as a cat leaping. (2) Extremely practical. (3) Princess Belinda was as lovely as the moon shining upon a lake full of water lilies. (4) And she was practical.

Answer 1 = ☐   2 = ☐   3 = ☐   4 = ☐

4. (1) Those declared medically unfit were refused entry. (2) New York was the main port of entry and it was here that they were subjected to medical examinations. (3) This must have been bitterly disappointing for people who had sacrificed so much. (4) Many Europeans set sail from Liverpool in search of a new life in the USA.

Answer 1 = ☐   2 = ☐   3 = ☐   4 = ☐

5. (1) They should sit down on the coaches and should leave them clean and tidy. (2) It is important that the students behave properly on coaches. (3) Students are then sitting in front of the tutors and are far easier to control. (4) Tutors should sit at the back of the coach.

Answer 1 = ☐   2 = ☐   3 = ☐   4 = ☐

6. (1) Then add these to the onions along with the garlic. (2) In a good solid saucepan, gently heat the olive oil and soften the onions in it for 5 minutes. (3) Fry for about 1 minute more, before adding the shredded cabbage. (4) Meanwhile crush the juniper berries by placing them on a flat surface and crushing them with the back of a tablespoon.

Answer 1 = ☐   2 = ☐   3 = ☐   4 = ☐

7. (1) It reached two main conclusions. (2) Second, the direction of migration changed – most migrants moving from rural areas to cities. (3) One of the first systematic surveys of migration in China analysed data for the years 1982–87. (4) First, that population migration increased between 1982 and 1987 when compared with earlier estimates.

Answer 1 = ☐   2 = ☐   3 = ☐   4 = ☐

8. (1) In a similar manner, glider pilots search for naturally rising streams of warm air called thermals, in order to gain altitude quickly. (2) Hot air balloons work on the same principle. (3) Convection is the upward movement of a pocket of warm air, which is at a different temperature from its surroundings. (4) As the air within the balloon is heated it becomes less dense and lighter than the surrounding air, enabling it to rise and lift the balloon with it.

Answer 1 = ☐   2 = ☐   3 = ☐   4 = ☐

9. (1) These are usually referred to as 'person specifications'. (2) However, many employers now recognize the necessity of specifying the qualities the job holder will need to meet the requirements of the particular job and to fit in with the organizational culture. (3) Job descriptions can be limited to brief outlines of work-related tasks rather than the personal attributes needed to be successful in doing the job. (4) They often distinguish between the attributes, skills and experiences that are *essential* for the job and those that are *desirable*.

Answer 1 = ☐   2 = ☐   3 = ☐   4 = ☐

10. (1) In addition, there has been a tendency to assume that the nub of the subject lies with children at school and not with the motivation of adult learners. (2) As a subject of study it is also divided across several disciplines and little synthesis has been undertaken hitherto. (3) However, in the past it has been sadly neglected by academics. (4) Motivation to learn is an urgent economic, social and political issue.

Answer 1 = ☐   2 = ☐   3 = ☐   4 = ☐

11. (1) The decision means that no one will be able to smoke in bars, restaurants or nightclubs north or south of the Irish border after that date. (2) The smoking ban also extends to private members' clubs and workplaces. (3) On hearing the news, the pro-smoking lobby was quick to promise that it would mount vigorous opposition to the implementation of the legislation. (4) Smoking will be banned in all public places in Northern Ireland from April 2007 according to a government announcement yesterday.

Answer 1 = ☐   2 = ☐   3 = ☐   4 = ☐

12. (1) Holiday work and placements can offer them an opportunity to develop marketable skills and experiences. (2) Experience of work is an increasingly important factor in the employment prospects of young adults. (3) This is because it enables them to gain insight into a particular employer or career and to see how this fits in with their hopes and aspirations. (4) Those experiences can also be very helpful in the process of discovering more about a job or career that suits them.

Answer 1 = ☐   2 = ☐   3 = ☐   4 = ☐

13. (1) It is important to distinguish between groups and teams. (2) However, it usually takes time to build genuine, supportive teamwork. (3) A group is merely a collection of individuals who come together to participate in a particular activity. (4) A group can become a team when the individual members collaborate and work together to achieve a common objective.

Answer 1 = ☐   2 = ☐   3 = ☐   4 = ☐

14. (1) However, the use of computers to handle and transmit large amounts of data is dependent on access to the internet. (2) Information and communications technology (ICT) is seen by many people as an opportunity for rural areas to overcome their major disadvantage – their remoteness. (3) Such work can now be done from home or from small offices in isolated locations. (4) Modern technology has removed the need for many office-based activities to be undertaken in urban areas.

Answer 1 = ☐   2 = ☐   3 = ☐   4 = ☐

15. (1) There are other people who decide what will be photo-graphed and how the resulting images will be chosen, rejected or edited to change the messages they convey. (2) However, the

artists, photographers and television crews who see for us beyond our range of vision are not the only filters between reality and us. (3) Instead we rely on printed and electronic images. (4) Through our own eyes we see only a little of the world, its people and its historical events.

Answer 1 = ☐   2 = ☐   3 = ☐   4 = ☐

The answers to the sentence sequence tests are given on pages 155–57.

9

Text comprehension tests

Introduction

In this type of verbal reasoning test you are given several prose passages, each of which is followed by a set of questions or incomplete statements related to its content. After reading a passage, your task is to choose, from the alternatives given, the best answer or answers to each question, or the best ending to the statement. In each case you are told the number (one or two) of answers required. It is therefore, a form of *multiple-choice test*.

The aim of tests of this type is to assess your ability to read and make accurate inferences from the text provided. It is because of this that this type of test is often called a *critical reasoning test*. You should not be surprised to find that you are unfamiliar with the subject content of the passages, the style in which they are written and the terms used by the authors. Part of the purpose of the test is to find out how well you can cope with unseen text that possesses these characteristics.

In each of the three practice tests you will find three extracts, each of which is followed by four questions (A to D), all of which offer you five alternatives from which to make your choice(s).

Read through the passage as carefully as you can, bearing in mind the time available. Then work your way through the multiple-choice items, putting ticks alongside what you consider to be the correct responses. Remember to put two ticks where you are told that there are two answers and one tick where you are instructed to give one answer. If you put fewer or more than the correct number of ticks for any of the items, your answer will be marked as incorrect. The shortened example given below should help you to understand what you have to do.

Example

Text extract
For almost 30 years, after it first captured nearly 50 per cent of the world market, Japan dominated international shipbuilding. Even during the 10-year period when the decline in shipbuilding in other countries had been exacerbated by the entry of South Korea into the global market, Japan managed to maintain its position. However, the cost was high. Japan's shipbuilders had to reduce their capacity by over one-third and to cut their workforce by almost as much as their counterparts in the United Kingdom. This created particular problems for Japan's large companies, because they were committed to lifetime employment for their employees. Although some of the surplus workforce were re-deployed in new industries and many others retired, it was difficult to absorb many more and the guarantee of lifetime employment, so crucial in Japanese industrial life, was put at risk.

A. The decline of the shipbuilding industry in Japan has
(2 answers)
1. been equivalent to that in the UK.
2. occurred despite the increase in its share of the world market.
3. resulted in a lowering of production costs.

4. had high social and economic costs.
5. threatened industrial relations in the country.

B. The world slump in shipbuilding was
(1 answer)
1. caused by Japan maintaining its output levels.
2. a result of Japan's policy of employment for life.
3. caused by the aggressive marketing of the South Koreans.
4. caused by a general decline in demand for new vessels.
5. the result of Japan's dominance of world markets.

Answers: A = 2 and 4; B = 4

Allow yourself 30 minutes to complete each test. When you have finished or the time is up, check your score by referring to the answers at the end of the book.

Text comprehension tests

Test 1

Text extract 1

It is clear that the ideal rural landscape for most people is not only a place of quiet retreat, harmony with nature and freedom from stress and technology, but is also 'olde worlde'. Around the belief that somehow life was better a generation or two ago has built up one of the two great rural myths. This is the concept of a 'golden age' when a contented pastoral way of life was possible for most people. In part it is a recollection of childhood, when the summers seemed brighter and the anxieties fewer, but also it is the 'magical evocation of a land that needs no farming'. That pastoral idyll found physical expression in the 17th-century and 18th-century French court, where nobles and their mistresses could play at being shepherds and nymphs with a few real sheep and stage-set cottages. In Victorian Britain, wealthy landowners built gingerbread-style cottages and Chinese dairies, but the picturesque homestead has never existed for the majority of rural dwellers. The second myth is that rural communities live in social harmony and interdependence, all 'harvest homes and dancing on the village green'. In fact, the lot of most agricultural workers (in the pre-industrial period) was miserable housing, an insecure livelihood and great dependence on the landowner. A more accurate picture of the modern village is farm workers living in council houses, and cottages occupied by weekending stockbrokers rather than that of a united land-tending community.

All this means that we have received a very strong cultural bias towards valuing and conserving landscape for its heritage, recreational and resource properties. At the same time, however, we rely on the countryside to provide us with food and raw materials: it is in this conflict that problems are to be found.

A. For the majority of people the ideal rural landscape is
(2 answers)
1. one of the two great myths about the countryside.
2. a place where stress is absent.
3. where people believe that life was better two generations ago.
4. quiet and old fashioned.
5. where nature and technology are in harmony with each other.

B. According to the author the idea of a 'golden age'
(2 answers)
1. evokes, as if by magic, a time when the majority of people could contentedly enjoy life in the country.
2. is based in part on people's memories of their childhood.
3. is the result of summers being duller today than they were in the past.

4.   can be explained by the fact that adults have fewer things to be anxious about than they did when they were young.
5.   is one of two great myths about the countryside.

C. In the passage the writer argues that
(2 answers)
1.   life for those who live in the countryside is all 'harvest home and dancing on the village green'.
2.   life in rural areas is idyllic.
3.   in country areas people live peacefully together and are mutually supportive.
4.   modern farm workers are unlikely to live in traditional country cottages.
5.   country cottages today are likely to be occupied only at weekends and by wealthy financiers.

D. The writer argues that
(1 answer)
1.   people do not want the countryside to be a living museum.
2.   people underestimate the value to society of the countryside as a recreational resource.
3.   the 'olde worlde' qualities of the countryside should be conserved for future generations.
4.   the countryside should be preserved as a place to which townspeople can escape from the stresses of modern living.
5.   there is a conflict between the widely held desire to conserve the countryside and the need to use it to provide primary products.

Text extract 2

London's phenomenal growth was probably at its fastest in the 16th century, a period when the population was growing everywhere. Many people were attracted to the rapidly growing port, which handled up to 90 per cent of total English foreign trade and gave rise to a wide range of ancillary industries. Others provided goods and services for the Court, which now settled permanently in the capital, and for the growing numbers of the rich and ambitious, who were attracted by the Court's presence. This concentration of the wealthy made London a great leisure centre and the main purveyor of professional services, especially in medicine and law. Population growth now tended to become cumulative. More people needed even more people to provide them with the goods and services that they required to survive in a large city.

London was always an unhealthy place and mortality rates were much higher than elsewhere in the country, sometimes rising to catastrophic heights, as in the terrible plagues of 1603, 1625 and 1665, the last of which probably killed 80,000 people, one-sixth of the total population of the city. Such high death rates, coupled with rather low fertility, meant that London could never grow by its own natural increase. In the century after 1650, when London continued to grow but the English population remained fairly stable, immigration to the city drained the countryside of people and gave London its highest-yet proportion of the total population. It was probably then, in the early 18th century London of Defoe and Hogarth, that the city also had its greatest significance as a cultural centre and as a school of manners and ideas for the rest of the country.

A. London's rate of population increase was at its greatest in the 16th century because
(1 answer)
1.   its death rate was the highest in Britain at that time.
2.   it was a time when the population was declining elsewhere.
3.   migrants were drawn there by the vast increase in trade passing through its docks.
4.   its high mortality rate was offset by a low birth rate.
5.   it had a high percentage of the country's total population.

B. In comparison to London, the population in the rest of the country in the 16th century was
(1 answer)
1. declining as a result of the disastrous effects of outbreaks of disease.
2. falling because of emigration to London.
3. also rising.
4. almost constant.
5. unable to grow naturally.

C. After 1600, the demography of London was characterized by
(2 answers)
1. high death rates and birth rates.
2. three major outbreaks of disease, the last of which was responsible for the deaths of over 80,000 people.
3. a rise in population through natural growth.
4. the continued movement of people into the city from rural areas.
5. population stability.

D. Examples of the economic hegemony of London in the 16th century include
(2 answers)
1. the movement of the Court permanently to the capital.
2. nine-tenths of England's overseas trade passing through its docks.
3. a large variety of secondary industries growing up around the port of London.
4. London becoming England's major intellectual and cultural centre at the time of Hogarth and Defoe.
5. the city becoming the major provider of professional and other services in England.

Text extract 3

The social catharsis that resulted from the Second World War gave an opportunity for economic, political and social reconstruction that was to be carefully designed. This was the promise: the world (which, as usual, meant Britain) was going to be a better place. Not only had fascism been 'defeated forever', there was a real chance to learn from all the hardships and upheavals of the 1930s and before. The Ministry of Information made great efforts to ensure that we 'win the peace'. And to get this message across, the government immediately enlisted the services of the design trade.

In the New Society, to be young was not only to be good: the emergence of the 'Youth Culture' in the 1950s offered princely possibilities of transformation. To transmit this promise, all forms of design were necessary – for behind the bold typefaces lay a new form of imperialism: the emergence of television and of an advertising industry, a system more pervasive than Hollywood had ever been. As Neil Postman wrote in *Amusing Ourselves to Death,* once there was 'no business like show business', but today the only business is show business. Design has been a prime agent in the compression of life into television time. A creative form, it quickly shifted its attention from social reconstruction towards the new post-war consumerism, imported from the USA. Superman comics and fast cars overtook the earlier promise. Design was soon forced to abdicate any distance its practitioners sought from the new world of advertising and entertainment. Rather than struggle to maintain their independence, most designers chose to conform.

A. The post-war government quickly engaged the design industry in order to
(2 answers)
1.   make sure that Britain was as successful during peacetime as it had been during the hostilities.

2.   complete the defeat of right-wing authoritarian dictator-
     ships.
3.   put into practice what had been learnt from the Second
     World War.
4.   ensure that its ideas were communicated effectively.
5.   sell the idea of the 'Youth Culture' to the post-war public.

B. The design industry was soon diverted away from rebuilding
post-war society by
(1 answer)
1.   creative opportunities offered by new technology.
2.   the emergence of a new group of consumers – young people
     with their own culture and purchasing power.
3.   ideas imported from the USA.
4.   pressure to conform.
5.   the commercial opportunities offered by advertising and new
     forms of entertainment.

C. The development of television and the advertising industry
(2 answers)
1.   provided munificent opportunities for change.
2.   rendered obsolete the idea put forward by Neil Postman that
     in the world of business 'show business' was unique.
3.   led to the emergence of the 'Youth Culture' of the 1950s.
4.   was far more powerful in its impact than the US cinema had
     ever been.
5.   enabled designers to distance themselves from the new con-
     sumerism.

D. Post-war Britain was subjected to neo-imperialism from across
the Atlantic in the form of
(2 answers)
1.   books by Neil Postman.
2.   imported fast cars.

3. a new emphasis on the production and purchase of goods and services.
4. the television and advertising industry.
5. a new-found independence for designers.

Test 2

Text extract 1

Up to now, all British political parties have assumed that the right magnets to try to move northwards are manufacturing industries, particularly of new-style consumer goods. This policy has never really worked, because it means trying to cajole private commercial enterprises to go to one part of the country when they know in their hearts that they would make bigger profits if they operated elsewhere. Unfortunately, in the near future this policy is likely to work even less well. The pull of Europe is calculated, for good economic reasons, to increase the flow of industry and population into the south-east. No government, whether Tory or Labour, could really bring itself to prohibit this movement into the British segment of the largest consumer-goods market in Western Europe. But in return, is there any major, non-manufacturing, non-market-located and really magnetic growth industry that could be safely and profitably transported north of the Trent? The most obvious candidate, despite the horrified cries of protest that will be sent up, is the industry of government itself.

London's past pride and present headache is to have become three capitals in one: the centre of commerce, finance and administration. In the 19th century, it was the financial capital and administrative capital only. The centre of gravity for industry and commerce in those days lay in the north. As industry has congealed into large corporate agglomerations, and as boards of directors have become financial tycoons rather than men of the workshop manager type, the centre of commercial power has inevitably moved down into the financial capital of the country. The financial mechanisms of the City of London could not be uprooted and shifted now, any more than the nearby continent of Europe can. But administration is something different, more detached, and (highly important) happens to be under the government's own control.

With modern means of communication it is no longer a handicap to have the administrative capital of a country separated from its financial capital. The USA, Australia, Brazil, Canada, The Netherlands, Switzerland and others have been separated; they have even found that there are certain governmental advantages in the fact.

A. At the time of writing the author foresees that
(1 answer)
1. the future trend will be towards a substantial increase in commercial and industrial activity in the north.
2. demographic trends will be towards an increase in the proportion of the population living in the south-east.
3. the administration of government, which is at present mainly conducted from London and the south-east, will one day be moved to the north.
4. as a consequence of the magnetic economic attraction of Europe, the financial institutions will one day have to move there.
5. in order to reduce the inflow of population to the south-east of the country, the government will one day introduce legislation to prevent industry moving into the region.

B. Successive Labour and Tory governments have
(1 answer)
1. considered it a disadvantage not to have the principal centres of administration and finance in the same place.
2. attempted to relocate the financial capital of the country in a region to the north of the River Trent.

3. adopted policies intended to coax firms making products currently in consumer demand to move out of the south-east.
4. shown manufacturing industry that the profits to be made in the north of the country are as big as elsewhere.
5. attempted to penalize manufacturing industries that have resisted pressure to move out of the London area.

C. The author points out that
(1 answer)
1. experience gained in a number of other countries indicates that effective government can be hindered if the administrative capital is separated from the financial capital.
2. the government is unable to exert any influence on where the centres of finance, commerce and administration should be located.
3. it would be a relatively simple matter for a government to reduce the magnetic attraction of the south-east to manufacturing industry.
4. the main centre of trade and industry in this country has not always been in the south-east.
5. there is no significant expanding industry not concerned with manufacturing that could be relocated in the north.

D. The centre of business has become established alongside the centre of finance in London because
(1 answer)
1. it is very close to the largest market for consumer goods in Western Europe.
2. it has been demonstrated in other countries that there are certain governmental advantages in having these two areas of activity centrally located.
3. changes in the structure and management of industry have placed the direction of industry in the hands of financial magnates.

4. little attempt has been made by successive governments to persuade industry to become established in any other part of the country.
5. companies can only make big profits if they are located in close proximity to the centre of financial power.

Text extract 2

Roehampton is probably the finest low-cost housing development in the world, and as it accommodates 9,500 people it is also one of the largest. A gloriously unspoiled 128 acres (formerly the grounds of five Victorian houses) adjacent to Richmond Park, provided an ideal site with superb trees and uneven topography. Every tree, every natural feature was used wherever possible. The building consists of a variety of high and low types, with large 10- and 11-storey 'point' (free-standing, high) houses and slab blocks accommodating more than half the population, and four-storey blocks containing maisonettes, roughly one-third. The other units are two- and three-storey terrace blocks and unusual buildings with single-storey one-room apartments for old people. There are altogether some 2,611 dwellings, with a population density of 110 people to a built-up acre. The 11- and 12-storey blocks, which visually dominate the entire development, are found on the high ground at both the east and west ends. The 25 'point' houses (each is a chubby rectangle in plan) have (in the newer west groups) two-bedroom and one-bedroom flats per floor. These tall, assertive blocks, well separated and beautifully landscaped, form three impressive groups as one walks or drives about on ever-curving roads. They are well planned inside and handsome outside. Nicely-scaled reinforced concrete panels, approximately 20 inches wide, cover them on four sides. All the apartments in these buildings are balcony-access two-bedroom maisonettes and are 12 feet wide and 38 feet deep including loggia. Raising them on stilts created wet weather play areas for children and absorbed the marked unevenness of the ground. Furthermore, the open see-through quality achieved by the use of stilts gives the buildings a lightness in the landscape. Like the tall 'point' houses, the slab-blocks are sheathed with pre-cast floor slabs and staircases. The four-storey blocks, the other major building type, also contain balcony access maisonettes, but these are wider than the apartments in the slabs and contain three bedrooms and a bathroom. The wonderful visual variety generated by these three major building types, and, to a lesser degree, the others, is one of the strong points in the pleasures of Roehampton.

A. The author considers that the site of the Roehampton housing development was ideal because
(1 answer)
1. the cost of building has been economical.
2. it was possible to include accommodation for the elderly.
3. the tract of land provided an uneven physical configuration, which was used as an attractive planning feature.
4. it was possible to build on land previously occupied by five old houses.
5. of the pleasant views that can be seen from the winding roads.

B. The effect of building the maisonettes off the ground has been to
(2 answers)
1. make them prevailing features in the landscape.
2. separate them from the blocks of high-rise flats.
3. create recreational space for children to use during inclement weather.
4. allow an open sight line that gives an impression of lightness to the construction.
5. provide a number of attractive walkways.

C. The predominant visual feature of the Roehampton development is
(1 answer)
1.   accommodation built off the ground on stilts.
2.   maisonettes with open galleries and balcony access.
3.   tower blocks of flats built on the highest ground.
4.   unusual small flats intended for elderly people.
5.   gently curving roads that follow the natural contours of the site.

D. One feature of the most recent buildings in the development is
(1 answer)
1.   that they provide apartments with three bedrooms and a bathroom.
2.   that they have been designed in a way that allows them to fit naturally with the uneven ground.
3.   the purposely built play areas for young children.
4.   a design that allows the residents to obtain balcony access.
5.   that they are covered by strengthened precast concrete panels.

Text extract 3

Although it is only within quite recent years that our knowledge has been well established of the significance of vitamins in food and of their specific nature and behaviour, it is nevertheless true that for many centuries what are now known as 'deficiency diseases' were in a vague uncertain fashion related to certain types of food. Thus it was recognized as long ago as the time of Chaucer that scurvy could be prevented or even cured by the addition of fruits and green vegetables to the diet of sailors and explorers. In 1735 Casali, in a description of the disease pellagra, noted in detail the deficiencies in the diets consumed in every case by the inhabitants of the districts in Spain where this disease was rife. In 1734 Bachstruv demonstrated that scurvy was due to nothing more than a total abstinence from fresh vegetable food and greens, for it could be cured by the addition of relatively very small quantities of these to a faulty diet. In 1747, James Lind, a naval surgeon at Haslar, divided 12 scurvy patients into six groups, and to each group made a different dietetic addition. The pair receiving oranges or lemons were quickly cured and scarcely less quickly those who had cider. He confirmed observations that had been made at the beginning of the 18th century that dried vegetables were useless against scurvy and adopted the view that 'no moisture whatsoever could restore the natural juices of the plant lost by evaporation'. He was also struck by the good effect of cows' milk in the treatment of scurvy, supposing it to be 'a truly vegetable liquor, an emulsion prepared of the most succulent, wholesome herbs'. Lind recommended that concentrated lemon juice syrup should be served throughout the Navy, but his suggestions were at first largely unheeded, so that in 1780 at least 2,400 men of the Channel Fleet were affected by scurvy, and the mortality exceeded that from battle and wounds. In 1793, on the persuasion of Dr Blane, the naval authorities made a trial of Dr Lind's suggestions as to the use of lemons. HMS Suffolk made a voyage of 19 weeks without touching any port; every man on board was given lemon juice and brown sugar in addition to his usual rations, and on arrival at Madras there had not been a single case of scurvy.

A. It was demonstrated as early as 1734 that
(1 answer)
1. scurvy could be prevented by eating desiccated vegetables.
2. there would be benefit in giving condensed lemon juice to all sailors.
3. scurvy was due to a lack of fresh vegetables and greens in the food eaten by sailors.
4. the drinking of cows' milk should be part of the treatment for scurvy.
5. oranges would be ineffective in the treatment of scurvy.

B. The Navy was persuaded to conduct an experiment in which lemon juice was to be served to sailors by
(1 answer)
1. an account of the inadequate nature of the food and drink regularly consumed by people living in particular areas of Spain.
2. an appreciation of the fact that a vitamin intake is an important part of a healthy diet.
3. the availability of a plentiful supply of fresh fruit and green vegetables.
4. the utilization by Dr Blane of proposals put forward by Dr Lind.
5. the non-stop nine-week voyage of HMS Suffolk to the Indian port of Madras.

C. The main purpose of this extract is to
(1 answer)
1. begin to trace historically a growing awareness of the significance of vitamins to a healthy diet.
2. bring to our attention the important voyage of HMS Suffolk.
3. show that the medical profession have been aware of cures for scurvy for a long time.
4. point out that in 1780 sailors were dying from scurvy because the naval authorities were unwilling to take notice of medical opinion.
5. show that moisture cannot replace the natural juices of a plant lost through evaporation.

D. In 1747 Dr James Lind
(2 answers)
1. established that a daily vitamin intake is an essential part of a healthy diet.
2. carried out a controlled medical experiment.

3. persuaded the naval authorities that a daily issue of concentrated lemon juice should be made throughout the Navy.
4. showed that fresh vegetables and greens could cure scurvy.
5. found that cider was almost as effective as oranges or lemons in curing scurvy.

Test 3

Text extract 1

Despair lies everywhere under the surface of British life today. It gives rise to bouts of cynicism, aggression and lack of interest in the outside world. This despair is caused by the rapid erosion of a traditional social order by a social revolution. One sort of ambition has died. But it has not been replaced by another. The pride that seemed so British in the 19th century – and which was traced to an aristocratic social structure by French observers such as Alexis de Tocqueville – has been eroded, without being replaced by the type of pride that de Tocqueville believed to be necessary in a society (such as France) that has rejected aristocracy.

Using de Tocqueville's ideas, it is tempting to suggest that Britain today is suspended between two social conditions – and that much of its malaise comes from the absence of an intelligible framework for individual ambition. In the early 1960s, Britain seemed to have found a 'middle way' between aristocratic and democratic attitudes – between a hierarchic and an individualist conception of society. But the unintended consequence of looking for a middle way has proved to be a moral confusion. Individuals no longer know what they are expected to do for themselves nor what will be done for them. What de Tocqueville called 'the Democratic Revolution' has stalled. We have lost the advantage of an aristocratic, without gaining the advantages of a democratic, social condition. Anyone trying to understand the condition of

Britain today – and the largest part of Britain is England – must start at this point.

De Tocqueville uses 'aristocratic' and 'democratic' to refer not merely to forms of government, but to types of society. In his view, an aristocratic society is defined by inequality of basic rights and conditions – the castes of feudal society being an extreme form – while he sees democratic society marked by relative equality of rights and conditions. The fixed social positions of the former create a powerful, self-confident elite resting on a permanently subordinated class. The dislodging of individuals from fixed positions in a democratic society releases individual ambition and raises expectations; it creates anxiety, competition and social mobility.

A. The writer suggests that de Tocqueville is of the opinion that (2 answers)

1. the terms 'aristocratic' and 'democratic' can be used to describe political, but not social, systems.
2. the degree of equality in a democracy is relative.
3. an aristocratic society is characterized by a rigid social order.
4. the greater equality of opportunity for social movement in a democracy leads to the concentration of power in a small hereditary group.
5. stress and rivalry are a consequence of subjecting individuals to the oppression of a caste system.

B. The writer suggests that contemporary Britain (1 answer)

1. lacks an understandable structure for personal aspiration.
2. has succeeded in its search to discover a middle course between alternative social structures.
3. is no longer in a state of ethical uncertainty.
4. has regained the 19th century self-esteem that it had lost.
5. unlike France, has discarded a social structure based upon the aristocracy.

C. According to the writer, the lack of hope that he detects in modern Britain
(2 answers)

1. is not ubiquitous.
2. causes British people to be narrow-minded and insular.
3. has resulted in the rapid destruction of the structure of society handed down from the past.
4. leads to outbursts of destructive behaviour and fits of sarcastic doubt.
5. is typical of a society that has turned its back on the nobility.

D. According to the writer, Britain's attempts in the 1960s to find a middle way
(2 answers)

1. are where anybody who is trying to make sense of the state of modern Britain should begin.
2. brought an end to democracy as defined by de Tocqueville.
3. resulted in the loss of the benefits that could have been derived from the retention of a hierarchical social system.
4. meant that people finally came to realize that they had to do more for themselves and rely less upon others.
5. deliberately created a moral dilemma.

Text extract 2

The atmosphere acquires moisture by evaporation from oceans, lakes, rivers and damp soil, or from moisture transpired by plants. Taken together, these are often referred to as 'evapotranspiration'. Evaporation occurs whenever energy is transported to an evaporating surface, as long as the vapour pressure in the air is below the saturated value. The saturation vapour pressure increases with temperature. The change in state from liquid to vapour requires energy to be expended in order to overcome the intermolecular attractions of the water particles. This energy is generally provided by the removal of heat from the immediate surroundings, causing an apparent heat loss (latent heat) and a consequent drop in temperature. Conversely, condensation releases this heat, and the temperature of an air mass in which condensation is occurring is increased as the water vapour reverts to its liquid state. The diurnal range of temperature is often moderated by damp air conditions – when evaporation takes place during the day and condensation at night.

Viewed another way, evaporation implies the addition of kinetic energy to individual water molecules and so, as their velocity increases, the chance of individual surface molecules escaping into the atmosphere becomes greater. As the faster molecules will generally be the first to escape, the average energy (and therefore temperature) of those composing the remaining liquid will decrease and the quantities of energy required for their continued release will become accordingly greater. In this way, evaporation decreases the temperature of the remaining liquid by an amount proportional to the latent heat of vaporization.

The rate of evaporation depends on a number of factors. The two most important are the difference between the saturation vapour pressure at the water surface and the vapour pressure of the air, and the existence of a continual supply of energy to the surface. Wind velocity can also affect the evaporation rate because the wind is generally associated with the importation of fresh, unsaturated air, which will absorb the available moisture.

Water loss from plant surfaces, chiefly leaves, is a complex process termed 'transpiration'. It occurs when the vapour pressure in the leaf cells is greater than the atmospheric vapour pressure, and is vital as a life function in that it causes a rise of plant nutrients from the soil and cools the leaves. Transpiration is controlled by the atmospheric factors that determine evaporation as well as by plant factors such as the stage of plant growth, leaf area and leaf temperature, and also by the amount of soil moisture. It occurs mainly during the day when the stomata (ie, small pores in the leaves) through which transpiration takes place are open.

A. When condensation occurs in the atmosphere
(2 answers)
1. the daily range of temperature (ie, the difference between the night-time minimum and day-time maximum temperatures) is always reduced.
2. energy is consumed.
3. the air becomes warmer.
4. water changes back from its gaseous to its liquid form.
5. energy in the form of heat is extracted from the air.

B. Evaporation
(1 answer)
1. is the means by which saturated air loses water vapour.
2. is the process by which water vapour is given off by the earth's water surfaces and growing vegetation.
3. is dependent upon energy being transported across the surfaces of oceans, lakes and rivers.
4. causes the temperature of the remaining non-evaporated water to increase.
5. results from the acceleration in the speed of movement of individual water molecules as the air temperature is proportionately reduced.

C. The rate of evaporation
(2 answers)
1. is related to the difference in atmospheric pressure in the air at and above the water surface.
2. is independent of the availability of a continuous supply of water at the earth's surface.
3. is unrelated to the speed of the air that moves across a body of water.

4. is influenced by the movement of dry air across the water surface.
5. increases with temperature.

D. Transpiration
(1 answer)
1. is less important to the survival of vegetation than evaporation.
2. is the means by which food is transported up through the plant from the soil.
3. results from the cooling of plant foliage.
4. occurs only during the day when the stomata, or small leaf-pores, are open.
5. is independent of the atmospheric factors that control evaporation.

Text extract 3

The Cabinet is the directing committee or board of management of British government. It is composed of Members of Parliament (including some from the House of Lords) holding office in the government. The size of the Cabinet has varied from 16 to 24, except for the War Cabinets of 1916–18 and 1940–45. In most cases, a member of the Cabinet is head of a major Department of State, bearing the title of Secretary of State. Some members of the Cabinet hold offices without heavy departmental duties, and their work is concerned either with advice or coordination at a high level, with the leadership of the two Houses or with special assignments (Lord President, Lord Privy Seal, Chancellor of the Duchy of Lancaster). The Prime Minister is chairperson of the Cabinet.

The Cabinet works through a system of sub-committees with the assistance of a small, but powerful, Cabinet Secretariat. The Cabinet Secretariat is the core of the administrative and advisory services that surround the Prime Minister and Cabinet, and owes its origin to the pressures of war. Until 1917, no Cabinet minutes were taken and, sometimes, ministers were uncertain what had been decided. The only official record was that sent by the Prime Minister to the Queen. Lloyd George changed this system by establishing a small team of civil servants to expedite the work of the Cabinet. Henceforth, the Cabinet Secretariat was responsible, under the Prime Minister, for preparing the agenda and supporting papers for Cabinet Meetings, making a record of the meeting and seeing to the initiation of action arising from Cabinet decisions.

The work soon developed into much more than simply the mechanical servicing of committees. Placing an item on the agenda may indicate not that it is too difficult or sensitive for any other body to decide, but rather that a decision has now been arrived at informally and requires the Cabinet's imprimatur. The Cabinet's business may thus be pre-processed so that Cabinet decisions can be arrived at quickly. The Cabinet Secretariat is involved in this pre-processing, trying to iron out disagreements and resolve conflicts. The Cabinet process itself may then be a registration of decisions already prepared through the network of departments and the Cabinet Office, of which the Secretariat is the central part.

A. As a consequence of a new method of conducting Cabinet business introduced by Lloyd George
(1 answer)
1. a formal report of Cabinet proceedings is sent to the Queen.
2. the Prime Minister takes the chair at Cabinet meetings.
3. the size of the Cabinet was increased from 16 to 24.
4. minutes are no longer taken at Cabinet meetings.
5. the work of the Cabinet is now carried out with greater efficiency.

B. Matters are generally brought before the Cabinet because
(1 answer)

1. a full discussion of all the relevant issues is required before a decision can be taken.
2. it is necessary to give official approval to decisions prepared in advance of the meeting.
3. there are often disputes and disagreements between departments that have to be resolved.
4. the decisions to be taken are often too substantial to be dealt with by lesser committees.
5. the Prime Minister requires an official record to send to the Queen.

C. The author suggests that efficient administration by the Cabinet Secretariat should mean that
(2 answers)

1. the Prime Minister is fully briefed on the work of all departments.
2. time is not wasted in taking decisions at Cabinet meetings.
3. the Cabinet is mostly concerned with ratifying decisions prepared in advance of the meeting.
4. sensitive items can be placed on the agenda.
5. the work of departments is coordinated at a high level.

D. In order to be a member of the Cabinet, it is necessary to be
(1 answer)

1. appointed to a post in the Cabinet Secretariat.
2. invited by the Prime Minister to be the head of a major government department.
3. elected to a seat in the House of Commons.
4. appointed to a government office bearing the title of Secretary for State.
5. a member of either the House of Commons or the House of Lords, and appointed to a government office.

Answers to the text comprehension tests are given on pages 157–58.

10

Verbal logical reasoning tests

Introduction

The verbal logical reasoning tests considered here are similar to those used in the selection of recruits to the police service. In this type of test you are given descriptions of imaginary events (or 'scenarios'), together with additional known facts. In each case they are followed by a set of conclusions that could be derived from the information provided. What you have to do is to consider each of the conclusions, and then decide if:

A.   The conclusion is *true* given the situation described and the facts that are known about it.
B.   The conclusion is *false* given the situation described and the facts that are known about it.
C.   It is *impossible to say* whether the conclusion is true or false given the situation described and the facts that are known about it.

In order to get a better idea of what you have to do, take a look at the example given below. Then *read* the information provided, *evaluate* each of the five conclusions, and *mark* your answer A, B or C in the answer boxes provided. When you have done that, check your answers against the ones given below.

Example

Scenario

Sarah Green, aged 10, and her friend from primary school Elizabeth Brown, aged 11, were reported to the local police station as missing at 7.30 pm on 10 June after they failed to return home from a visit to the local park to play on their skateboards. The police have set up a search party for the two missing girls. It is also known that:

- The park covers an area of 10 hectares and contains some very dense areas of trees and shrubs.
- Two girls were taken by ambulance to a local hospital at 6.30 pm.
- Sarah Green lived with her mother and stepfather.
- Elizabeth Brown was an only child living with her mother.
- Elizabeth had been given a new skateboard for her birthday.
- The park has a lake in addition to the wooded areas.
- Older students from a local secondary school had picked on Sarah on her way home from school.
- Elizabeth had regular sessions at school with a personal counsellor.

1. The two girls could have run away from home. ☐
2. The two girls had an accident in the park and were taken to hospital. ☐
3. The older students had picked on Sarah again in the park. ☐
4. Elizabeth had no brothers or sisters. ☐
5. Elizabeth had no personal problems either at school or at home. ☐

Answers

1 = A, 2 = C, 3 = C, 4 = A, 5 = B

In the verbal logical reasoning practice tests that follow, you will be given three fictitious accounts, each one accompanied by a list of known facts followed by a set of conclusions for you to consider. Although the information provided will be different in each case, when you have looked closely at a number of them you will begin to realize that they have many things in common. It is these common factors that provide you with 'clues' related to:

- *what* happened (ie, descriptions of imaginary events);
- *who* was involved (ie, information concerning the people involved);
- *when* the events took place (ie, dates and times);
- *where* the events were located (ie, names and descriptions of places and locations).

The ability to see the links in the text between these different types of information – and not to see them in isolation from each other – is vital if you are to succeed in this type of test. For example, in order to reach the right conclusion you may have to work out if a *person* could have been in a particular *place* where an *event* occurred at the *time* when it is known to have happened. The 'clues', which will enable you to get the right answer, will all be there in the text – all you have to do is to find them and interpret them in a way that is logically correct. However, just to make things a bit more difficult you will find that some of the information you are given is relevant to the conclusions you are being asked to reach, and that some of it is irrelevant. In fact some things might have been deliberately inserted to distract you and divert your attention away from the correct answer by taking you in the wrong direction.

You will also have to cope with information that has been presented in such a way as to lead you into making false assumptions. For example, you may be told that a person is known to have been inside a wine bar all evening and that he or she was seen to stagger and bump into someone on leaving. With this information it would be easy to assume that the person had been consuming alcohol and had staggered and bumped into someone for that reason. However, *given the situation described and the facts that are known about it*, there are other explanations that are perfectly logical. How many can you think of?

To do well in verbal logical reasoning tests, therefore, you have to be able to study the information provided with these things in mind – and under time pressure. So, here is a brief summary of what you should try to do:

- Read the information quickly to get an overall sense of what it is about – remember to ask yourself those important *'What?'*, *'Who?'*, *'When?'* and *'Where?'* questions.
- Try to separate information that is relevant from that which has been put there to distract you.
- For each item, scan the text again for the information you need to answer the question correctly.

Three practice tests of this type are given below. Each test contains four scenarios with five questions each – a total of *20 questions*; you should allow yourself *20 minutes per test*. Work as quickly and accurately as you can. If you are not sure of an answer, mark your best choice, but avoid wild guessing. If you want to change an answer, rub it out completely and then write your new answer in the appropriate box. Give yourself one mark for each correct answer and make a note of your scores to see if you are improving from test to test.

Verbal logical reasoning tests

Test 1

Scenario 1

Sixteen-year-old Susan Wood is a pupil at Oakfield Comprehensive School in Swinsford. With 580 pupils on the school roll, Oakfield is smaller than most other comprehensive schools. Susan is an exceptionally good artist and has won a national art competition that was sponsored by one of the leading banks. She is responsible for the artwork that appears in the school magazine, *The Oakfield Voice*. Susan is keen to work in marketing and is about to take her GCSE examinations. She then intends to go to Swinsford College of Further Education to take courses in Art and Business Studies. It is also known that:

- Susan is a member of the school choir and is taking guitar lessons.
- Susan lives with her mother, father and younger brother in a village on the outskirts of Swinsford.
- Susan's father is a maintenance engineer at an electronics factory.
- Susan works for eight hours a week, packing and stacking shelves at a local supermarket.
- Swinsford is a town in the Midlands with a population of about 175,000 people.

1. Oakfield is an all girls school. ☐
2. Susan is in her last year at Oakfield School. ☐
3. Susan is learning to play the guitar. ☐
4. Oakfield is an average size school. ☐
5. Susan walks to school. ☐

Scenario 2

Steve Pritchard is a plumber who works for Reliable Building Ltd. Reliable Building is a large company specializing in luxury flat development in the Greater London area. Steve was one of the plumbers completing a 10-storey block of flats in Richmond when an incident occurred. On returning to work after the weekend break it was found that because of a leak in the kitchen of the seventh floor flat, water had been running from the flat into the hallway and stairs and into the flats below. The total cost of the damage to carpets and other fittings was estimated at around £20,000. It is also known that:

- Steve is an experienced plumber.
- The last job that Steve had been asked to do before leaving the site for the weekend was to fit the bathroom of the flat in which the leak occurred.
- Steve had been keen to get away promptly at the end of the day because he was going away for the weekend.
- There had been an argument between Steve and the site foreman about the amount of overtime Steve had worked the week before.
- Steve had left his tools in the bathroom to finish the fitting after the weekend.

1. Steve was the only plumber working in the flat. ☐
2. Steve is one of several plumbers working on the site. ☐
3. Reliable Builders build mainly affordable starter homes. ☐
4. Steve was not concentrating on his work because of the argument with the foreman. ☐
5. Steve had finished fitting the bathroom. ☐

Scenario 3

Twenty-seven year old Tom Smith is a very successful long distance runner. Because he is classified as an elite athlete he receives financial support. When he was at school Tom won the European Junior Cross-country Championship. As an adult Tom has represented Great Britain on many occasions. His form has improved dramatically over the last two years. On the basis of coming third in the 10,000 metres at the European Championships and second in the marathon at the World Championships, he was selected to run in the 10,000 metres and the marathon at the Olympic Games. However, following random drug testing Tom was found to have taken a banned stimulant. It is also known that:

- Tom maintains his innocence and has appealed against the finding.
- Tom has been tested and found to be 'clean' on several previous occasions.
- Tom has been using a nasal decongestant spray.
- Tom is coached by a former East German coach who had links with athletes who have been banned for using performance-enhancing drugs.
- Tom claims his performance has improved because he can now afford to train at altitude in the USA.

1. Tom was given an illegal stimulant by his coach. ☐
2. Tom depends entirely on his winnings for his income. ☐
3. Tom had been the European Junior Cross-country champion. ☐
4. Tom was third in the marathon at the World Championships. ☐
5. Tom had been taking medication. ☐

Scenario 4

Mary Hayes was shopping with her partner Alan one frosty January morning. Their children, Fred, Sam and Charlie were at home being looked after by Alan's mother. Mary and Alan were taking advantage of the January sales to look for a new pair of shoes for Mary and a suit for Alan. After finding the items they wanted they called into a supermarket to get the week's groceries. Later, as they were walking back to the car park, Mary slipped on some steps and injured her arm and grazed her knee. Alan drove Mary to the local hospital where an X-ray revealed that she had broken her wrist. It is also known that:

- There was a handrail on the steps.
- Mary was carrying the sale items while Alan carried two large bags of groceries.
- Alan was walking in front of Mary.
- While in the supermarket Mary said that she was feeling dizzy.
- An elderly gentleman had fallen on the steps the day before.

1. Mary fell because the steps were slippery. ☐
2. Alan's mother was looking after the three children. ☐
3. The groceries were bought before looking for the items in the sales. ☐
4. Mary and Alan were unable to buy the suit and shoes they wanted. ☐
5. Mary was taken to the hospital in an ambulance. ☐

Test 2

Scenario 1

Mr and Mrs Cross were going to Portugal for a short mid-winter break. The journey to the airport took exactly 45 minutes and as the flight was at 5.15 am, and they had to check in at least one hour before departure, they arranged for a taxi to pick them up at 3.15 am. The taxi was late and they did not arrive at the airport until 50 minutes before the scheduled departure time. When they arrived at the airport they found that the flight was delayed because of a fault in the aircraft. The flight eventually left at 6.40 am and arrived in Faro, Portugal at 9.30 am. It is also known that:

- Because their luggage exceeded the weight allowance a surcharge of £22 had to be paid.
- While waiting to depart Mr and Mrs Cross were provided with complimentary coffee and doughnuts in the Airport Café.
- The couple had hired a small three-door car for the period of their stay in Portugal.
- Because of a medical condition Mr Cross does not drive.
- The hotel in which the couple were staying was close to the sea front.

1. The taxi arrived at the airport at 4.25 am.   ☐
2. The flight to Portugal took 2 hours 40 minutes.   ☐
3. The couple bought breakfast while waiting for the flight.   ☐
4. The taxi was late because the driver lost his way.   ☐
5. The hire car was collected at Faro airport.   ☐

Scenario 2

The Compton School is an above average size secondary school for pupils aged 11 to 16, situated on the outskirts of Brampton, a town in the West Midlands. Unemployment in the area has risen following a decline in motor manufacturing. In a letter to the local newspaper an angry parent was critical of the quality of education being provided by the school. The parent alleged his son was unable to learn because lessons were disrupted by poor behaviour and argued that this was the reason why the school's test and examination results are below national averages and well below those of most other schools in the area. It is also known that:

- Over the last six years the school has had three different headteachers.
- Two years ago a large part of the school was burnt down and many lessons take place in temporary classrooms while rebuilding work is going on.
- There are 1,200 pupils in the school, of whom 58 per cent are boys and 42 per cent are girls.
- The staff are coping well with the disruption being caused by the rebuilding work.
- The school was last inspected four years ago and judged to be providing a satisfactory quality of education at that time.

1. Employment in the area is rising. □
2. Lessons are disrupted by poor behaviour. □
3. The school is about the same size as most other schools. □
4. Test and examination results are below average because of the disruption caused by the rebuilding work. □
5. The present headteacher was the headteacher at the time when the school was last inspected. □

Scenario 3

Dr Ashwan Chander, a 38-year-old eye specialist living in Chelsea, West London, was meeting some friends for an evening meal at a restaurant in Kensington High Street. He saw his last patient at Hayes Green Hospital in Putney and left the hospital at about 6.00 pm. After walking to a florist shop to buy some flowers, he took a taxi to his mother's house in Fulham. He then intended to take another taxi from his mother's house to meet his friends at the restaurant at the agreed time of 8.00 pm. However, because the traffic was at a standstill, Dr Chander thought it best to walk and eventually arrived at the restaurant at about 8.20 pm. Later, when he went to pay the bill at the restaurant he found that he had lost his wallet. It is also known that:

- Dr Chander took money out of his wallet to pay for the flowers.
- Dr Chander did not take money from his wallet to pay for the taxi.
- The wallet was usually in Dr Chander's jacket, which he placed on the back of his chair in the restaurant.
- Police have been warning people to beware of pickpockets operating in the area.
- His credit card was used at 9.30 pm that night to pay for fuel at a garage in North London.

1. Dr Chander took a taxi from the hospital to Fulham. ☐
2. The wallet was last used when Dr Chander paid for the taxi. ☐
3. Dr Chander was late meeting his friends. ☐
4. A pickpocket stole the wallet as Dr Chander walked to the restaurant. ☐
5. Dr Chander walked to the restaurant because he could not find a taxi. ☐

Scenario 4

John and his partner Sarah are keen supporters of Midchester City Football Club and were travelling from Midchester to Oldfield to watch their team play in the FA Cup. The distance from Midchester to Oldfield is about 190 miles and John estimated that the travelling time would be about four hours. After they had been travelling for just under two hours they stopped for a break at a service station. On returning to the car they found that they had a puncture in one of the front tyres and so the wheel had to be changed. This took about 45 minutes. Shortly after leaving the service station they were stopped by a police patrol car for exceeding the speed limit. It is also known that:

- The driver passed a breathalyser test.
- The delay caused by changing the wheel had made them late for the start of the football match.
- Three years earlier John had his driving licence suspended for 12 months for driving while under the influence of alcohol.
- Sarah is a sales representative and has the use of a company car.
- It was raining heavily at the time the car was stopped.

1. The service station is about halfway between Midchester and Oldfield. ☐
2. Sarah was driving the car at the time it was stopped. ☐
3. The car was stopped about 80 miles from Midchester. ☐
4. The car was stopped because it was exceeding the maximum speed limit. ☐
5. John has previously been convicted of a speeding offence. ☐

Test 3

Scenario 1

At 3 am on 15 November the body of a young private soldier, Peter Adams, was found 25 kilometres south of Darlington, beside the railway line from Edinburgh to London. He was absent without leave from his army base where he was due to face a disciplinary hearing. A wallet found on his person contained a small sum of money, a family photograph, an identity card, an out-of-date service railcard and a single railway ticket from Edinburgh to Peterborough. It is also known that:

- The private had been drinking heavily and arguing with a fellow soldier, Mike Finnegan, in the buffet at Edinburgh station at 9.30 pm on 14 November.
- Adams had recently been seen at a disco in the company of Finnegan's 17-year-old daughter Susan, for whom he had been buying drinks.
- Adams and Finnegan had continued to drink and argue on the overnight train from Edinburgh to London.
- Finnegan was overheard to threaten Adams with a beating unless he stopped taking his daughter to discos and buying her drinks.
- Finnegan was seen to get off the train at Darlington at 1.45 am and head off from the station in the direction of the town centre.

1. Mike Finnegan is aged in his early 20s. ☐
2. Peter Adams had committed suicide by throwing himself off the overnight train from Edinburgh to London. ☐
3. Private Peter Adams was fraudulently travelling on the train from Edinburgh on the night of his fatal accident. ☐

4. The relationship Private Adams was having with Susan was the sole cause of the quarrel between him and Mike Finnegan. ☐

5. Mike Finnegan left the train at Darlington station in a panic in order to avoid detection for his part in the death of Private Adams. ☐

Scenario 2

At 7.20 pm, Sunday 23 November, a bicycle was removed from outside the video and off-licence store. A 14-year-old boy called James Gibb had left it there before going into the store to return a DVD he and his family had watched the previous evening. When he came out of the store the street was deserted, but he saw someone in the distance riding a bike in the direction of a nearby supermarket. The following facts are also known:

- The owner of the video and off-licence shop was serving inside the shop at the time the bicycle was stolen.
- A group of teenagers all wearing hooded tops were standing outside the store when James entered to return the DVD.
- The store closes promptly at 9 pm on Sunday evenings.
- The owner of the store is a man of strong opinions but has very poor eyesight.
- The person seen riding the bicycle was wearing a hooded top.
- James chatted for a few moments to the owner of the store before going back outside to retrieve his bicycle.

1. The owner was serving James inside the store at the time when the bicycle was taken. ☐

2. The owner was preparing to close the store for the evening when James arrived to return the DVD. ☐

3. The bicycle left by James in front of the store was stolen by one of the hooded teenagers. ☐

4. The owner gave the police a detailed description of the person he had seen through the window removing the bicycle from in front of the store. ☐
5. James was returning a DVD that his parents had borrowed from the store the previous evening. ☐

Scenario 3

A 72-year-old widow was said to be 'comfortable but in a state of shock' by a hospital spokesperson this morning. Mrs Susan Marsh suffered a head injury during the night when she disturbed an intruder who had broken into her ground floor flat on the Eastfield estate. This was the second time her home had been broken into in a month. In the first raid, the burglar broke a window and climbed in while Mrs Marsh was out for the evening visiting friends. The police believe that on this occasion the thief was disturbed when a neighbour returned home after walking his dog. It is also known that:

- Following the first break-in, workmen from the Housing Association boarded up the window to Mrs Marsh's flat.
- Mrs Marsh disturbed a man in her living room.
- When she returned home on the occasion of the first break-in Mrs Marsh found that nothing had been stolen.
- On the night Mrs Marsh suffered her head injuries the thief escaped with some valuable items of silverware and a small amount of ready cash.

1. On being wakened during the night Mrs Marsh went downstairs to investigate what had caused the noise. ☐
2. After being unsuccessful at the first attempt to rob Mrs Marsh's flat, the burglar broke in a second time. ☐
3. The intruder entered the flat by the same means on both occasions. ☐
4. The first break-in occurred when Mrs Marsh was out playing bingo and her neighbour was walking his dog. ☐

5. Although the burglar escaped with a small amount of
    cash and some silverware he failed to detect the money
    she had hidden in her bedroom.   ☐

Scenario 4

John Spark, a 32-year-old self-employed electrician, was given
a suspended sentence at Thirskston Magistrates Court together
with a fine of £1,000. Spark had been arrested and charged by the
police for a violent assault on a young man who was playing pool
with friends in a public house. It is also known that:

- The assault occurred following an argument that broke out
  between those playing pool and a group trying to watch a
  football match on television.
- A man called Martin Sore was treated on the evening of
  the assault at the Accident and Emergency Unit of the local
  hospital for a broken nose, bruised face and strained neck.
- Witnesses said that they had heard the complainant mocking
  John Spark about his private life.
- The landlord said that the argument which led to the assault
  had been a case of 'six of one and half a dozen of the other'.

1. The assault by John Spark took place in the poolroom
    of the public house where the incident took place.   ☐
2. The defendant John Spark was sent to prison and
    fined £1,000 at the Magistrates Court.   ☐
3. Martin Sore was treated in hospital for multiple injuries. ☐
4. Martin Sore had provoked the assault by mocking John
    Spark about his private life.   ☐
5. Two groups were involved in the argument in the public
    house, which led to the assault by John Spark.   ☐

The answers to the verbal logical reasoning tests are given on
pages 158–59.

Answers

Verbal usage tests (Chapter 4)

Test 1 (page 29)	Test 2 (page 36)	Test 3 (page 42)	Test 4 (page 49)
1. D	1. B	1. A	1. B
2. B	2. C	2. C	2. D
3. D	3. B	3. E	3. E
4. A	4. D	4. D	4. D
5. E	5. E	5. C	5. C
6. D	6. C	6. D	6. B
7. A	7. A	7. B	7. C
8. A	8. B	8. A	8. B
9. C	9. B	9. B	9. A
10. C	10. D	10. B	10. D
11. E	11. B	11. B	11. B
12. B	12. A	12. E	12. C
13. C	13. D	13. D	13. E
14. E	14. A	14. A	14. D
15. C	15. E	15. D	15. A
16. C	16. B	16. C	16. B
17. D	17. D	17. E	17. C
18. C	18. E	18. B	18. B

19. A	19. E	19. C	19. C
20. C	20. D	20. B	20. A
21. C	21. D	21. B	21. D
22. B	22. A	22. C	22. D
23. A	23. C	23. D	23. D
24. C	24. C	24. D	24. A
25. C	25. D	25. C	25. A

Word swap tests (Chapter 5)

Test 1 (page 58)

1. afloat; unconscious
2. greatest; highest
3. salad; supper
4. if; but
5. Before; while
6. ability; order
7. safety; shopping
8. make; provide
9. easy; sufficient
10. modern; housing
11. safety; use
12. future; task
13. demolished; otherwise
14. important; long
15. regret; matter
16. wave; spray
17. commercial; rapid
18. usually; long
19. scope; means
20. burst; passed
21. as; by

22. rhythm; rituals
23. environments; infinity
24. increasingly; off
25. relate; observe

Test 2 (page 60)

1. team; discipline
2. necessity; process
3. often; in
4. settlement; statement
5. resolve; number
6. advanced; estimated
7. diary; awareness
8. areas; graduates
9. witnesses; hypnosis
10. superior; craftsmen
11. abilities; attitudes
12. spending; veterinary
13. intervention; distribution
14. preferred; examined
15. experiments; dilemma
16. outskirts; south
17. coastal; man-made
18. methane; network
19. abuse; isolation
20. multi-storey; shopping
21. skills; purpose
22. water; shipping
23. acres; years
24. procedures; operations
25. control; practice

Test 3 (page 62)

1. reader; technique
2. providing; investigating
3. climax; 'blueprint'
4. professional; declining
5. private; sensitive
6. programs; recruits
7. refugees; stable
8. Electricity; pollution
9. production; wastage
10. professions; programmes
11. standard; problem
12. advent; problem
13. researchers; repeaters
14. vocabulary; primary
15. present; report
16. maintenance; pollution
17. numbered; employed
18. employment; equipment
19. making; closely
20. points; authors
21. greatest; rigorous
22. paste; nitroglycerine
23. replacing; commercial
24. television; flicker
25. killed; committed

Test 4 (page 64)

1. that; if
2. fortunately; although
3. expense; way
4. burden; disablement

5. acute; effervescent
6. cluster; regiment
7. system; possibility
8. breeze; day
9. eleventh-hour; growing
10. friendly; endangered
11. written; large
12. well; labour
13. transport; citizens
14. appoint; trade
15. organizations; meetings
16. service; survey
17. deals; complaints
18. costs; affects
19. future; new
20. doing; happening
21. number; body
22. processing; aiming
23. breeze; morning
24. factors; ideas
25. locating; unravel

Word links tests (Chapter 6)

Test 1 (page 68)

Left-hand words	*Right-hand words*
1. church	religion
2. radio	listener
3. picture	frame
4. mattress	sheet
5. individual	book
6. detergent	clothes

7.	idealism	realism
8.	record	turntable
9.	street	plan
10.	rural	countryside
11.	box	fight
12.	fences	horse
13.	fire	warming
14.	tongue	taste
15.	stone	peach
16.	law	court
17.	lock	door
18.	leaves	tea
19.	income	credit
20.	journalist	words

Test 2 (page 70)

Left-hand words	*Right-hand words*
1. cow	bush
2. ticket	concert
3. extra-time	match
4. top	milk
5. paintbrush	canvas
6. radio	television
7. reading	playing
8. banana	cabbage
9. cutting	writing
10. after	before
11. Scottish	English
12. over	above
13. window	wall
14. orange	tomato
15. education	health
16. badminton	shuttlecock

17.	silo	reservoir
18.	crowd	match
19.	monthly	salary
20.	arm	bracelet

Test 3 (page 72)

Left-hand words   *Right-hand words*
1.	basket	wastepaper
2.	innate	produced
3.	quarter	fifteen
4.	chess	pieces
5.	doctor	drugs
6.	transparent	opaque
7.	cub	wolf
8.	flock	sheep
9.	state	university
10.	end	finish
11.	stage	pitch
12.	Kenya	Africa
13.	water	sea
14.	family	team
15.	talk	write
16.	writing	reading
17.	years	weeks
18.	baby	adult
19.	sail	drive
20.	flower	chicken

Test 4 (page 74)

Left-hand words   *Right-hand words*
| 1. | lecturer | student |

2.	play	audience
3.	leaf	petal
4.	house	ship
5.	clown	circus
6.	illness	person
7.	law	music
8.	plane	pilot
9.	slow	fast
10.	musician	orchestra
11.	cub	cygnet
12.	radio	listener
13.	pipe	cable
14.	ink	pen
15.	skin	peel
16.	glider	sky
17.	herd	crowd
18.	tea	cup
19.	lawyer	client
20.	desk	office

Hidden sentences tests (Chapter 7)

Test 1 (page 79)

First three words	*Last three words*
1. keep; this; polythene	danger; of; suffocation
2. this; product; is	no; wood; pulp
3. fact; blurs; with	about; a; cameraman
4. I; found; it	so; lost; interest
5. studies; of; children	causes; of; conflict
6. in; Britain; the	has; gradually; diminished
7. one; big; bathtime	the; bathroom; floor
8. the; majority; of	are; expecting; visitors

9.	shopping; is; his	to; the; sales
10.	replacing; windows; is	can; easily; afford
11.	down; there; someone	the; tall; tree
12.	my; watch; stopped	town; hall; clock
13.	we; said; goodnight	left; as; usual
14.	historically; the; British	than; other; Europeans
15.	Sofina; is; a	what; she; wants

Test 2 (page 80)

First three words

Last three words

1.	he; stood; at	for; a; bus
2.	this; month; the	its; new; extension
3.	a; man; was	an; Industrial; Tribunal
4.	job; losses; in	for; many; years
5.	this; was; not	for; the; examination
6.	television; chat; shows	on; every; channel
7.	she; won; the	to; go; first
8.	more; information; about	spread; of; HIV
9.	the; whole; team	after; losing; narrowly
10.	sufficient; time; should	when; travelling; abroad
11.	all; fifth; year	do; community; service
12.	since; then; there	in; the; country
13.	as; he; talked	his; chest; expanded
14.	every; day; groups	around; the; cathedral
15.	I; love; to	in; the; morning

Test 3 (page 81)

First three words

Last three words

| 1. | we; were; closer | civil; war; yesterday |
| 2. | they; were; angry | on; the; motion |

3.	a; few; cars	new; number-plate (= two words)
4.	you; left; me	over; an; hour
5.	he; outlined; clearly	freedom; of; speech
6.	violence; is; threatening	of; best-selling (= two words)
7.	imagine; a; diet	as; you; like
8.	she; did; not	to; the; cinema
9.	the; appeal; court	all; thirteen; people
10.	I; intended; to	with; that; money
11.	we; recently; sent	must; now; pay
12.	for; decades; electricity	light; most; homes
13.	she; was; shopping	being; very; helpful
14.	water; exercise; classes	local; swimming; pools
15.	I; knocked; on	shout; come; in

Test 4 (page 83)

First three words *Last three words*

1.	he; was; punching	just; one; finger
2.	only; a; miracle	of; the; aeroplane
3.	Algeria; and; Morocco	French; colonial; government
4.	the; downstairs; of	a; dining; room
5.	the; conference; will	on; environmental; pollution
6.	oak; leaves; are	patches; on; them
7.	the; existing; runway	the; new; one
8.	variations; in; social	of; the; UK
9.	while; the; centres	spread; increasingly; outwards
10.	thousands; of; citizens	to; their; lives
11.	the; British; transport	the; changing; seasons
12.	the; headlines; used	difficult; to; understand
13.	many; employers; have	of; potential; employees
14.	there; are; many	uses; of; English
15.	like; any; other	number; of; situations

Sentence sequence tests (Chapter 8)

Test 1 (page 87)

Question	1	2	3	4
1.	4	2	3	1
2.	3	4	2	1
3.	4	2	3	1
4.	4	2	3	1
5.	2	4	1	3
6.	3	4	2	1
7.	3	2	1	4
8.	2	4	3	1
9.	4	1	3	2
10.	2	4	1	3
11.	4	1	3	2
12.	4	2	3	1
13.	2	4	3	1
14.	4	2	1	3
15.	3	1	4	2

Test 2 (page 91)

Question	1	2	3	4
1.	4	2	3	1
2.	3	1	4	2
3.	2	4	3	1
4.	3	4	2	1
5.	3	4	2	1
6.	2	4	3	1
7.	4	2	1	3
8.	2	4	1	3
9.	3	2	4	1
10.	2	4	1	3

11.	3	2	4	1
12.	3	2	1	4
13.	2	3	4	1
14.	4	3	2	1
15.	2	1	4	3

Test 3 (page 95)

Question	1	2	3	4
1.	2	1	3	4
2.	4	1	2	3
3.	3	1	4	2
4.	4	1	2	3
5.	3	2	4	1
6.	3	2	1	4
7.	3	1	4	2
8.	2	4	1	3
9.	1	4	3	2
10.	3	2	4	1
11.	3	2	4	1
12.	3	1	4	2
13.	3	1	4	2
14.	4	2	3	1
15.	3	1	4	2

Test 4 (page 99)

Question	1	2	3	4
1.	3	4	2	1
2.	4	2	1	3
3.	3	1	4	2
4.	4	2	1	3
5.	2	1	4	3

6.	2	4	1	3
7.	3	1	4	2
8.	3	2	4	1
9.	3	2	1	4
10.	4	3	2	1
11.	4	1	2	3
12.	2	1	4	3
13.	1	3	4	2
14.	2	4	3	1
15.	4	3	2	1

Text comprehension tests (Chapter 9)

Test 1 (page 106)

Extract 1	*2*	*3*
A = 2 and 4	A = 3	A = 1 and 4
B = 2 and 5	B = 3	B = 5
C = 4 and 5	C = 2 and 4	C = 2 and 4
D = 5	D = 2 and 5	D = 3 and 4

Test 2 (page 113)

Extract 1	*2*	*3*
A = 2	A = 3	A = 3
B = 3	B = 3 and 4	B = 4
C = 4	C = 3	C = 1
D = 3	D = 5	D = 2 and 5

Test 3 (page 121)

Extract 1	*2*	*3*
A = 2 and 3	A = 3 and 4	A = 5
B = 1	B = 3	B = 2
C = 2 and 4	C = 4 and 5	C = 2 and 3
D = 1 and 3	D = 2	D = 5

Verbal logical reasoning tests (Chapter 10)

Test 1 (page 133)

Scenario 1	*2*	*3*	*4*
1 = C	1 = B	1 = C	1 = C
2 = A	2 = A	2 = B	2 = A
3 = A	3 = B	3 = A	3 = B
4 = B	4 = C	4 = B	4 = B
5 = C	5 = B	5 = A	5 = B

Test 2 (page 137)

Scenario 1	*2*	*3*	*4*
1 = A	1 = B	1 = B	1 = A
2 = B	2 = C	2 = B	2 = C
3 = B	3 = B	3 = A	3 = B
4 = C	4 = C	4 = C	4 = C
5 = C	5 = C	5 = B	5 = C

Test 3 (page 141)

Scenario 1	*2*	*3*	*4*
1 = B	1 = C	1 = B	1 = C
2 = C	2 = B	2 = C	2 = B
3 = B	3 = C	3 = C	3 = A
4 = C	4 = B	4 = B	4 = C
5 = C	5 = C	5 = C	5 = A

Further reading from Kogan Page

Interview and Career Guidance

A–Z of Careers and Jobs, 13th edition, Susan Hodgson, 2006

Careers and Jobs in IT, David Yardley, 2004

Careers and Jobs in the Media, Simon Kent, 2005

Careers and Jobs in Nursing, Linda Nazarko, 2004

Careers and Jobs in the Police Service, Kim Clabby, 2004

Careers and Jobs in Travel and Tourism, Verité Reily Collins, 2004

Choosing Your Career, 2nd edition, Sally Longson, 2004

Great Answers to Tough Interview Questions, 6th edition, Martin Yate, 2005

How You Can Get That Job, 3rd edition, Rebecca Corfield, 2002

Preparing Your Own CV, 3rd edition, Rebecca Corfield, 2002

Readymade CVs, 3rd edition, Lynn Williams, 2004

Readymade Job Search Letters, 3rd edition, Lynn Williams, 2004

Right Career Moves Handbook, Sophie Allen, 2005

Successful Interview Skills, 4th edition, Rebecca Corfield, 2006

The Ultimate CV Book, Martin Yate, 2002

The Ultimate Interview Book, Lynn Williams, 2005

The Ultimate Job Search Book, Lynn Williams, 2006

The Ultimate Job Search Letters Book, Martin Yate, 2003

Titles in the Testing Series

The Advanced Numeracy Test Workbook, Mike Bryon, 2003

Aptitude, Personality and Motivation Tests, 2nd edition, Jim Barrett, 2004

The Aptitude Test Workbook, Jim Barrett, 2003

Graduate Psychometric Test Workbook, Mike Bryon, 2005

How to Master Personality Questionnaires, 2nd edition, Mark Parkinson, 2000

How to Master Psychometric Tests, 3rd edition, Mark Parkinson, 2004

How to Pass Advanced Aptitude Tests, Jim Barrett, 2002

How to Pass Advanced Numeracy Tests, Mike Bryon, 2002

How to Pass the Civil Service Qualifying Tests, 2nd edition, Mike Bryon, 2003

How to Pass the Firefighter Selection Process, Mike Bryon, 2004

How to Pass Graduate Psychometric Tests, 2nd edition, Mike Bryon, 2001

How to Pass the New Police Selection System, 2nd edition, Harry Tolley, Billy Hodge and Catherine Tolley, 2004

How to Pass Numeracy Tests, 3rd edition, Harry Tolley and Ken Thomas, 2006

How to Pass Numerical Reasoning Tests, revised edition, Heidi Smith, 2006

How to Pass Professional Level Psychometric Tests, 2nd edition, Sam Al-Jajjoka, 2004

How to Pass Selection Tests, 3rd edition, Mike Bryon and Sanjay Modha, 2005

How to Pass Technical Selection Tests, 2nd edition, Mike Bryon and Sanjay Modha, 2005

How to Succeed at an Assessment Centre, 2nd edition, Harry Tolley and Robert Wood, 2005

IQ and Psychometric Tests, Philip Carter, 2004

IQ and Psychometric Test Workbook, Philip Carter, 2005

The Numeracy Test Workbook, Mike Bryon, 2006

Test Your Own Aptitude, 3rd edition, Jim Barrett and Geoff Williams, 2003

The Ultimate Psychometric Test Book, Mike Bryon, 2006

CD ROMS

Psychometric Tests, Volume 1, The Times Testing Series, Editor Mike Bryon 2002

Test Your Aptitude, Volume 1, The Times Testing Series, Editor Mike Bryon, 2002

Test Your IQ, Volume 1, The Times Testing Series, Editor Mike Bryon, 2002